```
JC        Foster
71        Beres
P6
F6        The political
1984         philosophies of
             Plato and Hegel
```

$33.00

DATE			

+JC71 .P6 F6 1984

© THE BAKER & TAYLOR CO.

The Philosophy of Hegel

Seventeen of the most important
books on Hegel's philosophy
reprinted in sixteen volumes

Edited by
H. S. Harris
York University

A GARLAND SERIES

The Political Philosophies of Plato and Hegel

M. B. Foster

Garland Publishing, Inc.
New York & London
1984

For a complete list of the titles in this series
see the final pages of this volume.

This facsimile has been made from a copy in
the Yale Divinity School Library.

This reprint has been authorized by the Oxford University Press
Copyright Oxford University Press 1935, 1968

Library of Congress Cataloging in Publication Data

Foster, Michael Beresford.
The political philosophies of Plato and Hegel.

(The Philosophy of Hegel)
Reprint. Originally published: Oxford ; Clarendon
Press, 1935.
Includes index.
1. Plato. Republic. 2. Hegel, Georg Wilhelm Friedrich,
1770–1831. Grundlinien der Philosophie des Rechts.
3. State, The. I. Title. II. Series.
JC71.P6F6   1984   320.1'092'2   83-48506
ISBN 0-8240-5629-9 (acid-free paper)

The volumes in this series are printed on
acid-free, 250-year-life paper.

Printed in the United States of America

THE POLITICAL
PHILOSOPHIES
OF
PLATO AND HEGEL

OXFORD
UNIVERSITY PRESS
AMEN HOUSE, E.C. 4
London Edinburgh Glasgow
New York Toronto Melbourne
Capetown Bombay Calcutta
Madras Shangha
HUMPHREY MILFORD
PUBLISHER TO THE
UNIVERSITY

THE POLITICAL PHILOSOPHIES OF PLATO AND HEGEL

BY

M. B. FOSTER
STUDENT OF CHRIST CHURCH
OXFORD

OXFORD
AT THE CLARENDON PRESS
1935

PRINTED IN GREAT BRITAIN

To

THE PRESIDENT AND FELLOWS
OF ST. JOHN'S COLLEGE
OXFORD

*in gratitude for many benefits
which began with the award of a scholarship
and did not cease with its expiration*

PREFACE

THIS work purports to be an essay in the history of philosophy, and although I shall expose myself to an obvious rebuke if I attach a long preface to a little book, I cannot refrain from giving expression here to my conviction that, whatever may have been possible in past ages, there can be for us no genuine science of philosophy which is not based wholly on the study of the history of philosophy. I think, indeed, that the metaphor of basis and superstructure is inadequate to the intimacy of the relation between philosophy and the study of its history. It might be held to imply no more than that a study of the history of philosophy is an indispensable propaedeutic stage in the training of a philosopher, which he must have passed before his proper activity begins. I should make a higher claim for it than that. This study is not only indispensable to educate the judgement of one who is to philosophize sanely; it is the means by which he must continue to philosophize. To philosophize is to study the history of philosophy philosophically.

The general recognition of the higher of these claims might prelude a genuine renaissance of philosophy; the recognition at least of the lower is necessary to save it from disaster. Nothing but the discipline of historical study can preserve philosophy from both the opposite excesses of sophistry and mysticism. Nothing else can stem the progressive absorption, at least of professional philosophers, into one or other of the opposite camps of a 'Realism', in which all the rigour of scientific method is applied to a small and diminishing number of problems of purely academic interest, and of an 'Idealism', in which important subjects are treated indeed, but are treated as themes of a kind of imaginative speculation, of which even its devotees can hardly maintain that it is scientific. Neither method will produce a science of philosophy which is fit to rank, I will not say above but alongside the great disciplines, the natural and the other sciences, which together constitute the syllabus of modern knowledge; and if philosophy should come to the pass which I have anticipated, neither the brilliance of those who pursue it nor the prestige of its ancient name will save it for long from the disrepute which overwhelmed the Scholastic logic in the initial era of modern science.

It might be held that the disappearance of the class of professional philosophers would entail no great loss. Even now so much of the thought which has the best title to be called philosophical is contained in the works of authors who are primarily students of a science other than philosophy—theologians, mathematicians, natural scientists, or Platonic and Aristotelian scholars—as might well give a colour to the suspicion that philosophy is not itself a science at all, but a certain critical spirit or synoptic habit of mind, which can be exercised and developed only in the pursuit of a study other than itself.

I believe it indeed to be true that philosophical insight can be developed only in the scientific study of a definite subject-matter, and that all so-called methods of attaining philosophical truth apart from such a study are shams. But it will not follow that the professional philosopher has no legitimate employment, if it can be shown that there is a subject-matter which he alone is fitted to study. There is such a subject-matter, namely the great works which constitute the material of the history of philosophy. History of philosophy is not the study of histories of philosophy; that is history of philosophy at second-hand. It is a critical understanding of great philosophical works, being defective

PREFACE

in so far as either it is not critical or they are not great. If it is based upon such a study, philosophy may yet become a discipline which is more than academic in its interest without being less than scientific in its method; but I do not think that it is possible in any other way.

This contention will appear, perhaps, nearer to platitude than to paradox, if regard is had to the practice of contemporary professional philosophers. Of that great number who occupy a middle position, avoiding the extravagances of both the extreme parties which I have mentioned, there are few who would not regard the study of the history of philosophy at least as an indispensable part of the training of a philosopher; and there are few universities in this country whose philosophical teaching has any other basis. Contemporary philosophy is most strikingly differentiated from that of any previous age by the large space occupied by history of philosophy both in the writings of philosophers and in their teaching. But although the truth of the principle is confirmed by the conformity of so much of contemporary practice, it is still not superfluous to enunciate it. It is not enough that history of philosophy should be written and studied, if it is not written and studied philosophically; and this is hardly possible unless the historian has recognized that the study which he pursues is itself the science of philosophy. So long as he conceives it to be something distinct from, and inferior to, the activity of 'original philosophizing' (whatever in the world that may be), the work which he produces will in fact fall short of being genuinely philosophical. Laborious Histories of Philosophy, which chronicle without understanding, researches into the works of unimportant writers, whose chief recommendation to the researcher is that they have lapsed into oblivion: these are only extreme instances of the vice with which that misconception, until it is eradicated, must infect all history of philosophy to a greater or less degree. The existence of such unphilosophical history of philosophy then inevitably tends to perpetuate the misunderstanding of which it is the fruit, because the reader may be pardoned for refusing to believe, if this is history of philosophy, that philosophy is not something quite different. But it is not of such history of philosophy that it can be maintained that it is the genuine science of philosophy.

There is a further respect in which it may happen that history of philosophy suffers in esteem by being held responsible for what is really only a fault of some who practise it. It may suffer from the opposite defect of being too little laborious, so that when the work of the historian of philosophy upon, say, an ancient philosophical author is compared with that of the classical scholar upon the same material, it may well appear to be lacking in the firmness and precision which both qualify the study of the latter to be called a science and constitute its value as an educational discipline. The scholar who is accustomed to expend days of labour in extracting the meaning of a single passage, may be excused for thinking the method of that historian superficial, whom he observes to run from Thales to Aristotle in an hour and a half and with no trouble at all.

I suggest that history of philosophy is open to this damaging comparison if, and in so far as, it endeavours to study ideas without an exact knowledge of the works in which they have been expressed. But such a study stands to genuine history of philosophy only in the relation in which, say, a superficial 'history of culture' would stand to genuine criticism. Both suffer from similar defects, to be cured by similar means. History of philosophy becomes critical only in so far as it adopts a method as rigorous as that of the scholar. This is not to say that it must adopt the same method, or that philosophy is possible only upon a basis of

PREFACE xi

scholarship (although the striking success achieved by the school of philosophy which arose in Oxford mainly on this foundation, is a sufficient indication of the affinity between them); but only that a philosophy which seeks to be scientific should take as its model the exactitude of the scholar rather than that of the mathematician.

I should be sorry if the value of the method which I have advocated were to be estimated by my own success in carrying it out; but I must leave the defects of my execution to the judgement of the reader. The design of the book is to this extent more limited than the title implies, that I have confined my attention not only to two philosophers, but to two works: the *Republic* and the *Philosophy of Right*. I have tried to write a book which may be intelligible (except for the footnotes and appendices) to a reader who has not studied these two works in the original languages, and I have endeavoured to consult his convenience by appending a glossary (p. 205) giving the nearest English equivalents of Greek words which I have transliterated but not translated in the text; but I have not attempted to write a book for the use of a reader who has not studied them at all.

A good deal of the book, especially of the earlier part, has been anticipated in lectures given in Oxford in 1932 and 1933, and some points in the criticism of Hegel in a work written in Germany for a doctorate of the University of Kiel and published in 1929 under the title *Die Geschichte als Schicksal des Geistes in der Hegelschen Philosophie*. That the form in which it is presented is not more imperfect than it is, is due to the rigorous standards of Mr. R. G. Collingwood, who saw it in his capacity as Delegate of the University Press. In several places the argument also has, I think, been strengthened by the attempt to meet his criticisms. The task of revision was lightened for me by

Mr. J. D. Mabbott, who read the whole of the original draft, and gave me the benefit of his criticisms and suggestions; and by others who read parts of it. I wish to thank them for this assistance, and Mr. J. G. Barrington Ward for his kindness in undertaking the labour of correcting the proofs.

I cannot assess the extent of my indebtedness for the ideas in the book, but two works from which I have at different times derived much stimulus are Bosanquet's *Companion to Plato's Republic* and J. Stenzel's *Plato der Erzieher*; and I hope that those who have been my teachers in these subjects, namely Professor J. L. Stocks, Mr. Mabbott, Mr. H. W. B. Joseph, in his lectures on the *Republic*, and Professor Richard Kroner, will accept my thanks and this acknowledgement for whatever they recognize as theirs.

OXFORD, M. B. F.
March 1935.

TEXTS AND ABBREVIATIONS

I HAVE used the Oxford text of the *Republic* and G. Lasson's of the *Philosophie des Rechts* (2nd ed., Leipzig, 1921). Where I have added a page number to quotations from the latter work, the reference is to the paging of Lasson's edition. The letter A ('Anmerkung') after a paragraph-number (as, for example, § 279 A) refers to the explanatory notes added by Hegel to the text of the paragraphs in the edition of the work published by him. The letter Z ('Zusatz') refers to the extracts from reports of Hegel's lectures, printed together on pp. 284–371 in Lasson's edition, but distributed throughout the text by Gans and by Dyde in his English translation.

CONTENTS

I. THE POLIS AND THE STATE AS OBJECTS OF POLITICAL PHILOSOPHY . . 1
   APPENDIX A. Plato's confusion of the threefold division of the Polis with the division of labour . 36
   APPENDIX B. Is the product of the 'second education' to be νομοθέτης or φύλαξ? . . . 37

II. DIKAIOSUNE AND FREEDOM IN PLATO 39
    APPENDIX C. Education and government in Plato 70

III. HEGEL'S CRITICISM OF PLATO: THE 'SUBJECTIVE ELEMENT' . . 72
     APPENDIX D. The virtue of Sophrosune in Plato 99
     APPENDIX E. Hegel's criticisms of Plato, together with other references to 'subjective freedom', &c., their ambiguity 101

IV. LAW AS THE CONDITION OF FREEDOM IN THE STATE 110

V. 'CIVIL SOCIETY' AND STATE IN HEGEL 142

VI. RULER AND SOVEREIGN . . . 180

GLOSSARY 205

INDEX 206

I

THE POLIS AND THE STATE AS OBJECTS OF POLITICAL PHILOSOPHY

IF we ask, What is the object of political philosophy? or What is political philosophy about? the answer is in one sense simple. We can say at least that Greek political philosophy is concerned with the Polis and that modern political philosophy is concerned with the State.

The difference between the two is sometimes expressed by saying that Greek political philosophy dealt with the City-State, whereas modern political philosophy deals with the Nation-State. I wish to avoid that terminology, because it suggests that the State differs from the Polis only by the accident of its geographical extent. That suggestion is false. The Polis was not a miniature State; and it will be one of my objects to show that it lacked, or exhibited at most imperfectly, the characteristics which essentially constitute what we call a State, and to derive from these deficiencies those peculiar characteristics of ancient political philosophy which distinguish it from its modern counterpart.

Nevertheless, I wish at present to consider the character which State and Polis have in common, the character in virtue of which they are, or have been, both objects of the same branch of knowledge, namely of political philosophy. The answer to this question also is in no doubt. Polis and State have both been made objects of political philosophy because, whatever their differences, they are both forms of political association. It will be necessary to raise the question what the distinctive character of political association is, and it may be useful as a preliminary to dismiss two other conceptions of association which lack this distinctive character.

In the purely physical world, according to the view of it assumed in what is now called the 'classical' physics, material particles are capable of aggregation so as to form different material bodies. But it is the nature of the particles, not the nature of the aggregates, which is the object of scientific knowledge. Not tables and chairs, but the atoms of which they are composed, are the proper objects of physics. If the principle by which men are associated to form political communities were not different from that by which, on this theory of the physical world, atoms are aggregated to form material bodies, there could be no proper object for the study of political philosophy. The nature of men would be a possible object of scientific knowledge, but not the nature of cities or of states.

In the world of organic nature a different form of association is found. An organism is composed of its members, but not in the same way in which a physical body is composed of its material atoms. The principle of an organic unity seems to be that its elements are associated together in virtue of their differences from one another. The organs of a living creature 'belong together' in such a way that we can call the totality of them not an aggregate of members, but a single animal, only because the members are different from each other and reciprocally complementary in virtue of their differences. The product of such an association possesses, as a mere aggregate of identical physical particles does not, a nature of its own which is a proper object of scientific understanding. A wasp or a sponge has a nature which can be studied by biological science.

This type of organic unity is found in all living things, but it is also found elsewhere than in the individual organism. It is found, for example, in animal societies. A multiplicity of bees may be associated together in such a way that we can speak of them no longer as a mere multiplicity, but

OBJECTS OF POLITICAL PHILOSOPHY

in the singular number as forming 'a hive', and this unity obviously depends upon the differentiation of its constituent members and the specialization of their functions. The organic unity of animal societies, like the organic unity of individual living creatures, is an object of biological science, although, may be, of a different branch of it.

If human beings were organized into communities by no other principle than this of organic unity, human associations would be the proper object of a natural science. But the existence of a study such as political philosophy, which is something other than a natural science, presupposes that its objects are constituted by a principle other than that of organic unity. The product of an organic unity is still a natural object, but the peculiarity of political philosophy presupposes that its object is more than a natural, namely a spiritual[1] object. But if the products of political association, the Polis and the State, are more than natural objects, their members must be associated together by something more than an organic unity.

It is important to emphasize this point because so many recent political philosophies (especially 'idealist' philosophies) have stressed what they call the organic nature of the State. They have seen in the specialization of labour an example of the differentiation of function and have

[1] I am aware that 'spirit' is a dangerous term to use. I shall employ it as the contradictory of 'nature', and shall endeavour to give it a fuller connotation later in this chapter (p. 26 *inf.*). That it is dangerous is a reason for using it with caution, but is not a reason for not using it. It is, besides, no more dangerous than its correlative 'nature'; because either of a pair of correlatives is necessarily infected by an obscurity in the conception of the other. It is impossible to be clear about the meaning of 'up' so long as you are in any doubt of the meaning of 'down'. The greater danger to clear thinking comes from those who light-heartedly use the term 'nature' without even realizing that it implies a correlative. And yet the implication of this unexpressed correlative is precisely what gives to the term 'nature' the peculiar meaning which differentiates it from the Greek term $\phi\acute{v}\sigma\iota s$.

regarded the reciprocal dependence of the various trades and professions as the tie which unites human society. We must repeat that if human society exhibits no other tie than this, then there is no meaning in calling it 'political' society, and no justification for setting it apart as the object of a science which claims to be different in kind from biological, or any natural, science, namely political philosophy. Animal societies are held together by ties which differ from this not in kind, but only in degree of complication. A hive of bees is held together by the reciprocal dependence of its members, and if a society of men is held together by nothing else, then the structure of human society will be a proper object not of any so-called political philosophy, but of biological science, because it will not exhibit a different kind of unity from that studied by biology, but will only supply one further example of the same kind.

In the argument of Plato's *Republic* the conclusion is implicit, though not expressed, that the Polis does exhibit a third type of unity, which makes it more than an organism, and constitutes it a proper object of political philosophy.

I repeat 'which makes it more than an organism', because to assert this is not to deny that the Polis is organically one. None of the forms of unity which I have mentioned excludes the subordinate forms, but is super-imposed upon them. Thus every living creature is at the same time a material body, composed of material particles interacting according to mechanical laws, and to say that the unity of a living creature is organic is not to deny to it the nature of a material body, but to assert that it exhibits over and above this a unity which is more than that of a material body.

Similarly if we claim that human society is, or may be, political, that is not to deny that such a society will exhibit

OBJECTS OF POLITICAL PHILOSOPHY

the forms of animal association, but only to claim that it will exhibit a further form of unity as well. Every man is at the same time an animal, just as every living creature is at the same time a material body; and so every political society will possess at the same time an animal or natural basis or substructure.

Thus there is no inconsistency between the assertion that the Polis exhibits an organic or natural unity, and the claim that its unity is more than organic. It is possible for Plato both to maintain that human society involves an association of reciprocal dependence for the satisfaction of the needs of life and to imply that such an association does not of itself constitute anything which can properly be termed a Polis, or a form of political association.

The difficulty with Plato is that, while he asserts the former, he only implies the latter, and never clearly realizes that the implication will carry him far beyond his original assertion; or perhaps more accurately that he continually asserts the political unity of the Polis, without any recognition whatever that he is doing more than repeat his original assertion of its organic unity.

Thus there are two lines or currents in Plato's argument, the former explicit, the latter implicit; the former contending that the Polis exhibits an organic, that is a natural, unity, the latter implying that it is essential to the Polis that it should possess over and above its natural unity a differentia which no natural object can possess.

I will sketch briefly these two lines in Plato's argument. The former, the argument that the Polis is (at least) an organic unity, is to be found in the account of what is commonly called the 'first city' of the *Republic*.[1] Plato calls this the account of the 'becoming', as opposed to being, of the Polis; it is intended to show how a Polis comes into

[1] ii. 369a–372d.

being,[1] not what its being essentially is.[2] This distinction is not one with which we are immediately familiar; we should represent it to ourselves, I suggest, as the distinction between the animal basis of all human association and the further characteristic, peculiar to the association of rational animals, which, when it supervenes, renders their society more than animal and distinctively political.[3]

We shall be able to judge of this suggestion better when we have seen what Plato says. 'A Polis comes into being because each individual man is not self-sufficient, but lacking in many things.'[4] Each man has varied requirements, such as those for food, clothing, and shelter, but each has only a limited capacity to supply these requirements. Almost any man may be a skilled farmer or a skilled weaver or a skilled builder of houses, but no man can be all these, and each is therefore dependent upon others for the supply of the necessities to which his own skill does not reach. This mutual dependence is the universal bond of human association; even four or five men united by this tie constitute something which is a Polis in germ.[5]

Clearly the unity of such a society is of the type which we have called organic. It depends upon the different capacities of its individual members to satisfy the needs of life, and it would at once be dissolved if these differences were

---

[1] γιγνομένην πόλιν. ii. 369a.

[2] Cf. the same distinction in Aristotle: πόλις ... γινομένη μὲν τοῦ ζῆν ἕνεκεν, οὖσα δὲ τοῦ εὖ ζῆν. *Politics*, i. 2.

[3] Or perhaps the etymological affinity of γίγνεσθαι with γένος may help to elucidate Plato's meaning. Man is animal by genus and rational by differentia; and so the Polis is by genus a form of association based on animal needs, by differentia a form of political association (what this qualification implies has, of course, still to be determined). Thus the account of the γιγνομένη πόλις, the determination of the genus, is the first part of that grand definition of the Polis *per genus et differentiam* in which the main argument of the *Republic* consists.

[4] ii. 369b.   [5] ἥ γε ἀναγκαιοτάτη πόλις. ii. 369d.

OBJECTS OF POLITICAL PHILOSOPHY

annulled. Four or five men of the same trade would not constitute even the germ of a Polis, but would remain a multiplicity of individuals. The unity of the whole depends upon that specialization of individual function[1] with which we are familiar as division of labour.

Plato completes the sketch of the 'first city' by developing a little further this principle of the division of labour. Thus the farmer will not be able to make all his own tools, but these will be made for him by craftsmen who specialize in their making, and so there arise the further trades of smiths and carpenters. But this increasing complication is merely an extension of the principle of organic unity, and not the introduction of another principle.

When the sketch is complete, Glaucon makes the famous comment that this is a 'city of swine'.[2] He makes it, it is true, solely in reference to the simplicity of diet which Plato prescribes for his citizens, but his criticism may fairly be extended to the plan of this city as a whole. It does exhibit no characteristic which is not to be found in an animal community, and its unity is not different in kind from the unity displayed by natural organisms.

This city is not, of course, that ideal Polis which it is the main theme of the *Republic* to define. That Polis differs from it in certain important respects, and if we can decide what these are, we shall have a clue to the question which we have not so far attempted to answer: What constitutes the differentia of a political association and makes it a proper object of political philosophy?

Plato conceives the ideal Polis as developing out of the 'first city', and we must consider shortly his account of the development.[3] The distinctive characteristic which he

[1] ἓν ἔργον ἕκαστον πράττειν, τὸ τὰ ἑαυτοῦ πράττειν. See iii. 394e, 397e, 406c, e; iv. 433a, 441e.   [2] ii. 372d.
[3] ii. 372e ff.

attributes to the 'first city' is what he calls 'health'.[1] We may paraphrase this term as 'balance' or 'harmony'. It is that co-ordination of the trades or arts[2] one with another which is the bond of their unity, but which it is not the function of any one trade to produce, just as the health of a living body is not the function of any one organ within it, but consists in the balance of all the organs and the adjustment of their functions to one another.

The first step in the process by which the 'first city' is developed into the ideal Polis consists in the loss of this primitive 'health'. We must go on, says Plato, to examine the city 'not only in its process of coming to be, but also in a state of fever'.[3] This state of fever consists in a derangement of the balance of functions which characterized the primitive community. This derangement, Plato thinks, is caused by the growth of luxury, which multiplies a man's wants, and with them the classes of artisans required to provide for them, until at last it exceeds the capacity of his own community to supply them. When this point is reached, the community is driven to attempt to supply its own deficiencies by attacks upon its neighbours, and thus in this fever of the city Plato finds the genesis of war.[4]

The community will not only attack its neighbours. If they are suffering from a fever like its own, it must expect attacks from them, and the necessity of defending itself from these assaults gives rise to the formation of an entirely new class within it, additional to those which it has already, the class, namely, of warriors or guardians, which shall 'sally forth and fight to the death against the assailants on behalf

---

[1] ii. 372e ἡ μὲν οὖν ἀληθινὴ πόλις δοκεῖ μοι εἶναι ἣν διεληλύθαμεν, ὥσπερ ὑγιής τις. Cf. 373b ἐκείνη ἡ ὑγιεινή. . . .   [2] τέχναι.
[3] ii. 372e τρυφῶσαν.
[4] ii. 373e. On this point cf. further, p. 35 *inf*.

OBJECTS OF POLITICAL PHILOSOPHY

of the life of the city and of that organization which we have just been describing'.[1]

Plato assumes without hesitation that the function of defending the city, like the functions of farming or shoe-making or the supply of any other need, must be assigned to a special class, and he appeals to the principle of the division of labour, which he has already enunciated, to support his assumption,[2] but it is vitally important to realize that the function of defending the city is not really comparable to the function of supplying this or that want of its members. The function of a warrior is not to supply a want; it is to preserve the integrity of that balanced system within which wants are supplied. The specialization of warriors into a class is at least no ordinary application of the principle of the division of labour, because the function of the warriors is nothing but the preservation of that division and of the harmonious adjustment of organs which depends upon it.

The principle which is at stake here will become clearer if we follow the further development in Plato's conception of the guardian class. When they are first introduced the only function of the guardians is to fight in defence of their fellow citizens against external enemies, and Plato seems only gradually to feel his way to the conclusion that this class, or a further subdivision of it, must be entrusted with a more important function still, the function of ruling.[3]

---

[1] ii. 374a, freely translated.   [2] ii. 374a–e.
[3] The whole account of the training of the warriors in σωφροσύνη in iii. 389d–390d, presupposes but does not assert the existence of a separate class of ἄρχοντες, to whom the warriors are subject (389e ἀρχόντων μὲν ὑπηκόους εἶναι, αὐτοὺς δὲ ἄρχοντας τῶν περὶ πότους καὶ ἀφροδίσια καὶ περὶ ἐδωδὰς ἡδονῶν). In iii. 398b the whole scheme of education hitherto discussed is referred to as the education of στρατιῶται, a term which seems more definitely than φύλακες to imply ἄρχοντες as its correlative. In iii. 405a we are told that the τρυφή of the city will give rise to the special classes of physicians *and expert judges*. The expert judges can be none other than the ἄρχοντες, who have yet to be introduced

THE POLIS AND THE STATE AS

This subdivision of the guardian class follows from the recognition that the functions which it must perform are essentially not simple but dual. It must preserve[1] the balance of the primitive community against disturbance not only from without but from within. The necessity of the latter, as of the former, function becomes evident in the 'fevered' state of the city, because the 'fever' not only provokes the irruption of external enemies, but causes (or rather *is*) a derangement or disorder of the internal balance, and the guardians' work of preserving the city must take the double form of repelling the assaults from without and of remedying the disorder within.)The former task is appropriated to the warriors, the latter to the rulers, and because the disorder which the rulers have to prevent or cure consists either in the failure of one trade or section of the state to fulfil its proper functions, or in the invasion by one section of the province of another,[2] it is natural that the first function recognized as demanding the presence of a separate class of rulers should be government, in the sense of penal repression of disorder.[3]

as a separate class (cf. iii. 409a, and iv. 433e ἆρα τοῖς ἄρχουσιν ἐν τῇ πόλει τὰς δίκας προστάξεις δικάζειν;); in iii. 412a the implication is for the first time explicitly drawn, that the whole course of education so far prescribed for the warriors implies the presence of an ἐπιστάτης, and we are told (412b) that we must accordingly distinguish rulers from ruled within the guardian class itself. Plato proceeds to describe the tests upon which this κατάστασις τῶν ἀρχόντων (414a) must proceed, and henceforth this class of ἄρχοντες (variously designated φυλακώτατοι πόλεως (412c), φύλακες παντελεῖς (414b), τέλεοι φύλακες) is explicitly recognized as a third element within the Polis.

[1] Or restore. [2] πολυπραγμοσύνη.
[3] δικάζειν, v. iii. 405 ff., and cf. iv. 433e ἢ ἄλλου οὑτινοσοῦν μᾶλλον ἐφιέμενοι δικάσουσιν ἢ τούτου, ὅπως ἂν ἕκαστοι μήτ' ἔχωσι τἀλλότρια μήτε τῶν αὑτῶν στερῶνται. We ourselves often use the phrase that the primary function of government is to 'keep order', but we rarely pause to reflect what order it is to keep, or what constitutes disorder. Plato has defined what order is to be maintained: that which subsisted naturally in the 'first city'.

OBJECTS OF POLITICAL PHILOSOPHY 11

A second and more important line of thought which leads Plato to the same conclusion is the following: having decided that there must be a special class of fighters charged with the defence of the city, he sees that the individuals composing this class must be qualified to perform this task not only by the natural endowment of a warlike temper,[1] but by a course of training,[2] both in the arts and in bodily exercises,[3] which shall direct their natural disposition to the ends which it is intended to subserve, and develop it into civic courage,[4] instead of allowing it to degenerate, as otherwise it inevitably would, into a promiscuous quarrelsomeness. This introduces the discussion of the education of the guardians (still conceived exclusively as fighters) which occupies the greater part of Books ii and iii.[5] Having sketched in some detail the course of training to be prescribed for the fighters, Plato points out that if this training is ever actually to be carried out, there must be somebody within the city capable of prescribing it.[6] He has shown that the production of a character suitable to a defender depends upon the due admixture of humane studies and bodily exercises as ingredients of his training. It is not necessary that the subject of this training should know the proportion in which these ingredients are combined, or the reason why this proportion is the right one, and it constitutes no part of his proper excellence that he should do so. In order that the civic virtue of Andreia may be produced in him, it is necessary that the proportion should be right, but not that he should be convinced of its rightness or aware of what makes it right. But the trainer who is to produce this character must himself possess a further excellence beyond that which

---

[1] ii. 374e ff.
[2] ii. 376c; cf. iv. 430b, for an explicit denial that the ἀνδρεία of the guardians can be ἄνευ παιδείας.   [3] μουσική and γυμναστική.
[4] πολιτικὴ ἀνδρεία, iv. 430c.   [5] ii. 376e–iii. 412a.
[6] iii. 412a.

it is the object of his training to produce. He must *know* the proportions in which the elements of education are to be mingled in order to produce the character required. Thus the production of a class of fighters in the state necessarily presupposes the existence of a further class which is competent to prescribe their training, and this is the class of rulers in the strictest sense.

We may thus arrive at the necessity of a subdivision within the guardian class by either of two lines of thought, but whichever line we follow, the distinctive excellence which must characterize the class of rulers will be found to be the same. If it is to prevent disorder within the city and thus to preserve or to restore that good order or harmony which was the 'health' of the primitive city, it must know on what this harmony depends and in what that good order consists. If it is to train defenders of the city against external enemies, it must know the principles which are to inform their training. The excellence which it must possess is insight, knowledge, or wisdom.[1] This excellence is not the knowledge required for the pursuit of any particular art or trade, but knowledge of the balance of the particular trades and of the order by which the different artificers are united in a single association; it is not technical knowledge but political wisdom. Nevertheless, Plato applies his old principle of the division of labour in specializing this knowledge in a single class.[2]

In following this argument we have so far laid most stress upon the reasons which necessitate the distinction of the rulers as a separate class from those other guardians whom Plato henceforth calls 'auxiliaries'; but it must not be forgotten that this separation is only a subdivision within the

---

[1] σοφία.
[2] Cf. further pp. 29 ff. *inf.*; and for references to the *Republic*, Appendix A, p. 36 *inf.*

OBJECTS OF POLITICAL PHILOSOPHY

guardian class. Since the ideal Polis, which is a political association, differs only by the inclusion of this class from the 'first city', which is not, we shall find in the function of the guardian class a clue to Plato's answer to the question which we began by asking: What is the differentia of political association? To understand this function presupposes an understanding of the great Greek distinction between Form and Matter.

Form is the principle which constitutes not only the identity of an object with other objects of the same kind, but the unity which enables it to be regarded as itself a single object. Thus the form of a table is that essence which is comprehended in its definition, and is, in this case, equivalent to its end or purpose. This form is not only identical in all tables, but is the principle of unity in each. It is that which so orders the indeterminate multiplicity of the sensible 'matter' that the various sensible qualities cohere together to constitute a single object. This particular colour, those particular tactual qualities of hardness and smoothness, have in their own nature no affinity with one another. They 'belong together' only in so far as the form, plan, or design of a table demands the compresence of them all, and so links them one with another that the resulting unit can be designated by a singular noun. No object is possible or conceivable except as such a union of form with matter; and of these two form is universal and intelligible, matter is particular and sensible.

In a product of art, such as a table is, the information, by which the object is constituted, is the work of the artist, and his work is guided by the intelligent apprehension of the universal form to be embodied. In a natural object the form is present, but it is not necessary for its presence that it should have been previously conceived. In a living and growing natural object the form is that which controls its growth, and the maintenance of which constitutes its well-being or health.

Health is the preservation of the form of the living body, but to preserve it is not the function of any particular bodily organ. One organ can produce sweat, another gastric juices, and so on; but no organ can produce health, which depends on (or rather which *is*) the balance or harmony in the functioning of all the organs. Nor need the form be previously known in order to be realized as the health of the body; only when health has failed, and has to be artificially restored by the physician, is it necessary that a knowledge of the form should precede its restoration. But the restored health is no more than the primitive health of the undoctored body the function of any single bodily organ. It is the work of reason, or of purpose guided by reason, and exercised, further, not by the body restored to health, but by the physician who cures it. A body restored to health by the art of a physician is something not to be met with in the realm of nature; and though we suppose a sick man to be his own physician and to restore his own health by a conscious apprehension of the form to be realized, the restoration is none the more a natural process, nor the result one which a mere organism could achieve. It presupposes something more than the functioning of his organs, namely an activity of reason, which can be the work of no organ, since it has to control the work of all.

We have made use before of the analogy of a living organism to illustrate Plato's 'first city', in which each trade corresponds to a bodily organ and the unity of the whole to the unconscious health of the body. But in the transition from the 'first city' to the fully developed Polis the unity has been threatened and consciously restored. The class of guardians has been introduced with no other task than to preserve this unity. Their task is no longer analogous to the

OBJECTS OF POLITICAL PHILOSOPHY 15

functioning of any particular bodily organ, but to the activity of reasonable purpose, for which health is the conscious object.[1] The analogy of an organic body cannot be extended from the 'first city' to the ideal Polis;[2] for in the ideal Polis a class has been introduced which is not comparable to an organ, because its end is not the performance of a function, but the maintenance of that balance of functions which is the health of the city and the 'form' unifying the various activities of its constituent elements.

We may return to the question which we began by asking: What is the peculiar character of a *political* society, which differentiates it from the forms of association to be found in the realm of nature and constitutes it a proper object (not, e.g., of biological science, but) of political philosophy? We suggested that we might find a clue to the answer (or at least to Plato's answer) if we could discover what differentiates the fully developed Polis of the *Republic* from the 'first city', and now one grand distinction between them is clear. In the 'first city' the form which constitutes its unity (division of labour and harmony of trades) is natural in the sense that it is primitive and the product of no conscious purpose. In the ideal Polis this identical form is restored, and its justice depends entirely upon the condition that the form restored shall be identical with the natural one; but the process of its restoration is an act informed by conscious purpose.

The ideal Polis is thus identical with the 'first city' in that its form is prescribed by nature; it differs from it in that it

[1] Strictly speaking, the form of the city is conscious object not for the guardians as such, but only for the rulers.

[2] If we attempted to extend it, we should have to confess that the only analogue of the Polis would be a strange and monstrous growth in which in some unimaginable way reason was localized in a new and unprecedented organ. Plato himself, when he passes from the 'first city' to the ideal Polis, replaces the analogy of the living body, implied in the metaphor of health, by the analogy of the human soul, which, whatever it is, is not an organism.

is imposed by art. Whereas the members of the 'first city' were imagined to be united in accordance with a certain form,[1] the members of the ideal Polis are held in unity by *knowledge* of the form.

This is no trivial difference,[2] but one which introduces a principle of association different from any which we have hitherto considered. We must guard in particular against the misapprehension that the knowledge of the form which is characteristic of the ideal Polis is no more than an epiphenomenal consciousness, merely *accompanying* the restoration of the balance which the fever in the city had disturbed. On the contrary, knowledge of the form must precede this restoration, and in any city which has emerged from its state of primitive innocence, the unity and harmony which make it a city can be maintained only on the strength of such knowledge. The knowledge can no more be epiphenomenal than the medical knowledge of a doctor is epiphenomenal to the recovery of a patient whom he has cured; or the potter's knowledge of what a vase is used for, to the process of moulding the clay.

All unities in nature, that is, all natural objects, depend upon the presence of a form. The unity of a Polis depends, as no natural unity depends, but as the unity of the products of art depends, upon that form's being known. The form of the ideal Polis is always existing, because it has an eternal being in the realm of ideas, but it is actualized only if and when a ruler ascends to the knowledge of it and realizes it in an earthly city in virtue of this knowledge.

---

[1] The organic unity of the whole.

[2] Compare the distinction drawn by Kant between actions determined in accordance with a law and actions determined by the conception of a law, the former being natural, the latter moral. Failure to observe this distinction is the defect of Spinoza's conception of freedom. He defines freedom as the understanding of laws by which human conduct is determined equally whether they are understood or not.

OBJECTS OF POLITICAL PHILOSOPHY 17

The Polis is more than a natural object by that which assimilates it to a product of art, namely by the fact that its form can be realized only by being known; and the recognition of this peculiar characteristic of political society constitutes Plato's permanently valuable contribution to political philosophy.

Plato, it is true, never formulates in so many words even this theory of political society. He promulgates no distinction either between natural science and philosophy, or between a natural and a political association. There are passages in the earlier books of the *Republic* in which he clearly conceives the organization of the ideal Polis to differ from that of the 'first city' *only* by defect; that is, only as the state of a man recovered from fever differs from that of a man who has never succumbed to it.[1] Nevertheless, the work as a whole demands the abandonment of this conception. The ideal Polis makes possible, as the 'first city' does not, the realization of the virtues of the ruler and the auxiliary. It must therefore possess a perfection of its own, which the 'first city' does not possess, and this peculiar perfection can be none other than that character which we have described. We are justified, therefore, in calling Platonic the ascription of this character to political society.

But if it is Platonic to follow the implications of the argument thus far, it is no less Platonic to refuse to follow them further. It is equally Platonic to assert that the form of the Polis is imposed by a conscious activity, and to deny that the form itself is determined or in any way affected by this activity;[2] to assert that ruling is an imposition of order directed by reason, but to refuse to assert that it is the

---

[1] *v.*, e.g., iii. 405*a–c*.
[2] Plato's whole defence of the 'Justice' of the Polis depends upon his contention that its form is 'natural', in the sense that it is not altered in the ideal Polis from what it was in the primitive community.

imposition of an order upon the ruler's self. These further implications must in fact be drawn; the presence within the ideal Polis of an organization for imposing and maintaining its form makes the form itself of the Polis different from that of the primitive city; and the mere fact that the rulers themselves are included as a class within the city which they rule necessitates that the order which they maintain in the city must be an order imposed upon themselves. To draw these further implications is to move at a bound from the sphere of Greek to that of modern political philosophy; and the root of the main contradictions and confusions of Plato's theory will be found in his failure to draw them.

Both the positive achievement of the Platonic conception and its limitations appear most clearly in his doctrine that ruling is an art, or Techne;[1] for it is characteristic of a 'technical' activity in the Greek sense of the word both that it should issue in the realization of a design which is itself unaffected by the process of realization, and that it should impose a form upon a material which is other than the craftsman's self. We must pass to a brief consideration of the doctrine of ruling from each point of view, both from that of its achievement and from that of its limitations.

Form is, as we have seen,[2] both universal and intelligible. Ruling, which is the realization of form, is therefore an activity both directed towards the embodiment of a universal and controlled by a precedent intellectual apprehen-

---

[1] τέχνη: the same Greek word which I translated 'trade' or 'craft' when it was used to describe the constituent elements of the primitive community. No wonder that the use of such a word should make it easy for Plato to ignore the fact that in introducing a ruling class he is introducing a different principle of association. The 'first city' was essentially an organization of τέχναι, and to add a class of rulers is only to add one τέχνη more. See p. 12 *sup.*, and Appendix A, *inf.*, p. 36.

[2] p. 13 *sup.*

OBJECTS OF POLITICAL PHILOSOPHY

sion of the universal to be embodied. The analogy with a Techne illustrates both of these characteristics with an unsurpassed lucidity. For, in the first place, the work of the craftsman, in so far as he is a craftsman and is not diverted from his proper end, is directed and controlled by the form which it is to realize. His purpose is never captivated by a detail in his work, as though the detail could be in itself an end, but is directed upon the plan of the whole, and upon the detail only so far as it is demanded by the plan. The craftsman who is carving a figure must carve it to particular dimensions; this limb, let us say, must measure three feet, no more and no less, that angle must measure precisely forty-three degrees. But if he supposes that there is anything intrinsically excellent in a length of three feet, if he has a preference for this angle because it contains forty-three degrees, and not because that particular measurement is demanded by the total effect, i.e. in so far as he regards the particular as good not simply as embodying the form, but intrinsically, he is to that extent no craftsman.

In the second place the analogy enforces the second essential characteristic of the ruler's (though not also of the warrior's) function, namely that the ruler, like the craftsman, must possess antecedently to his work a clear scientific insight[1] into the form which his work is to realize. Thus the analogy with Techne illustrates both the generic nature and the specific differentia of the activity of ruling: it is directed to the realization of a universal, and it is informed by the intellectual apprehension of the universal to be realized.

Because the universal is apprehensible only by reason, while its realization is an act of will, the comparison of ruling with a Techne implies as the ideal of action in a ruler an activity in which will is wholly subordinate to reason.

[1] ἐπιστήμη.

In one respect, indeed, the ruler achieves this ideal with a completeness which his analogue, the craftsman, cannot attain. The craftsman attains it *in so far as he is a craftsman*, that is to say, in so far as his energies are absorbed in realizing in his material a design comprehended by his reason. But it is not given to any craftsman to be a craftsman and nothing else. He has physical fears to be stilled and bodily wants to be satisfied; to supply them, he must be a Chrematistes, or money-maker, as well as a craftsman.[1] His liberty to apply himself to his craft is dependent upon the condition that its products supply a demand or fulfil a want. Once his task is set him, reason governs his performance; but the setting of his task depends on an *order* (whether of master or of customer), which, as it arises from caprice, is addressed not to his reason, but to the irrational part of his nature. The order of a master addresses itself to his fear, and he is then a slave. To the order of a customer he is submitted by his bodily wants and the consequent necessity of supplying them by his earnings; and to Plato this submission was no less a slavery. He had no conception that economic wants exhibited a form of reason in being subject to the operation of economic laws, and therefore he could see no difference in principle between the subjection of the craftsman to the demands of the consumer and the subjection of the slave to the caprice of the master. Both relations alike seemed to subordinate the activity of reason to the irrational; the craftsman is rational in performing the task set, but the task is set for him by an appeal either to his fear or to his cupidity. But the end of the ruler's activity, which is the form of the Polis, is the object of no want, because it is the form within which all wants and the processes of supplying them are systematized and ordered. The universal system of desires and their satisfactions can be the object of no desire, but

[1] Cf. i. 346.

OBJECTS OF POLITICAL PHILOSOPHY

only of reason, and thus the end of the ruler's activity, and not merely the means, is set by reason.

The conception of the ruler's activity which Plato developed by the Techne analogy: of the activity, namely, in which every other element of the soul is subordinated to reason, is the model from which almost every subsequent ideal of moral conduct has been, more or less directly, derived.

So much for the value of the Techne analogy, and the doctrine of the Polis which it implies; we have now to observe its fatal limitations. We have to show that it belongs to the essence of a political society to possess not only the property which the analogy emphasizes, that its order is imposed by reason, but also the further property, which the analogy by implication denies, that its order is self-imposed; that this second property is implied by the first; and that Plato himself in the *Republic* is driven by the irresistible logic of this implication to a position inconsistent with the doctrine of the Polis which we have sketched above, and only concealed the full extent of this inconsistency from himself by a confusion of concepts in reality distinct.

It is essential to the conception of Techne that it is the imposition of form by the 'demiurge', or craftsman,[1] upon a material other than himself. This limitation, inherent in the nature of the activity, is the only reason why the presence of the guardians is required at all. (The 'first city' is composed of craftsmen, each employed in the imposition upon his material of the form proper to his craft.) If it belonged to their craft to impose a form not only upon their material but upon themselves, they could themselves restore the harmony among the crafts which the fever in the city disrupts. It is because the very nature of their activity precludes this reflection upon themselves that another set

[1] δημιουργός.

of craftsmen is required, who shall impose, or re-impose, an order upon the Technae, as these in their turn impose order upon their own material. This order is, of course, the organization of the various Technae, which is the form of the community. The 'technical' activities of the particular crafts are the matter upon which it is imposed, and thus the craftsman, who in respect of the products of his own craft 'wills the universal' or form, can will only the matter or the particular, and not the form, of the community of which he is a member.

To will the form of the community, i.e. to impose the organization of the division of labour upon the matter of the particular Technae, is the exclusive function of the rulers. The activity of these partakes itself of the nature of a Techne, in that they in their turn impose a form upon a material *other than themselves*. Thus we find in the ideal Polis that the specialization of function by division of labour, which is the form to restore which the guardians were introduced, is in fact maintained in the subject or producing class, but is carefully and most rigorously excluded from the class of guardians by the regulations for the community of wives and property. The ruler, a true demiurge, imposes an order to which he is not himself subject.

But the guardians (rulers and warriors) themselves constitute classes within the Polis. If they are to form a unity, as they must, with one another and with the subject class, they must be organized into such a unity by the imposition of a form. The form of this organization is clear; it is that triple organization of classes which characterizes the ideal city. But what demiurge imposes this form, the form of which the diverse bodies of the subjects, the warriors, *and the rulers themselves* are only the matter? The answer to this question lays bare the whole weakness of the Techne doctrine of ruling: this form is clearly imposed by the crafts-

OBJECTS OF POLITICAL PHILOSOPHY 23

man who constructs the ideal Polis and determines its constitution, i.e. by Socrates and the interlocutors who cooperate with him in the dialogue. It is 'we', as Socrates says, who are 'founders of the city';[1] 'we' are the lawgivers who establish the constitution by which the functions of the rulers and their relations to the ruled are themselves determined;[2] 'we' must understand the principle upon which this constitution is based, but the rulers do not need to understand it, and Socrates actually recommends in one passage[3] that it should be concealed from them. 'We', finally, are not ourselves members of the Polis which 'we' found, nor subject to the constitution which 'we' lay down.

So far we have simply been following out the consequences of the Techne theory of ruling. If ruling is an art and the ruler a demiurge, he must presuppose the activity of a founder or lawgiver to construct the constitution within which his 'art of ruling' may be exercised. Precisely at this point the weakness of the theory becomes apparent to Plato himself. For the part of founder is played, as we have seen, by Socrates and his collaborators, who construct the ideal Polis in virtue of their philosophical insight into the principles involved. But a Polis so constructed, a city which is the product merely of a philosophical speculation, can possess no more than an ideal being. It must necessarily lack reality; and it is the recognition of this consequence, thrust forcibly upon him by Glaucon,[4] which induces

---

[1] ii. 378e: καὶ ἐγὼ εἶπον ˙Ω 'Αδείμαντε, οὐκ ἐσμὲν ποιηταὶ ἐγώ τε καὶ σὺ ἐν τῷ παρόντι, ἀλλ' οἰκισταὶ πόλεως.

[2] iii. 398b: . . . ἐν ἐκείνοις τοῖς τύποις οἷς κατ' ἀρχὰς ἐνομοθετησάμεθα, ὅτε τοὺς στρατιώτας ἐπεχειροῦμεν παιδεύειν. Cf. iii. 417b, iv. 429e–430a, v. 458c Σὺ μὲν τοίνυν, ἦν δ' ἐγώ, ὁ νομοθέτης αὐτοῖς; and v. 471b τιθῶμεν δὴ καὶ τοῦτον τὸν νόμον τοῖς φύλαξι . . .; et passim.

[3] iii. 414b, c τίς ἂν οὖν ἡμῖν, ἦν δ' ἐγώ, μηχανὴ γένοιτο τῶν ψευδῶν τῶν ἐν δέοντι γιγνομένων, ὧν δὴ νῦν ἐλέγομεν, γενναῖόν τι ἓν ψευδομένους πεῖσαι μάλιστα μὲν καὶ αὐτοὺς τοὺς ἄρχοντας, εἰ δὲ μή, τὴν ἄλλην πόλιν;

[4] v. 471c.

Socrates to break off abruptly from any further particularization of the constitution of the ideal Polis, and embark upon the train of argument which leads to the introduction of the 'second education' of the *Republic*.

On what conditions can the ideal Polis be realized? Clearly only on condition that the task of founding it is withdrawn from the speculative philosopher, the result of whose speculations can never be more than a Utopia, and assigned to a class of rulers within the Polis itself; or, alternatively, if the class of rulers within the city can be endowed by education with that insight which the speculative philosophers (Socrates and Glaucon) possess into the principle which determines the relation (not only of trade to trade within the class of tradesmen, but) of class to class, and consequently of their own class to that of their subjects. Socrates expresses this condition when he says 'there must be included within the city a definite class of it, which possesses the same insight into the principles of the constitution which you, Glaucon, possessed in your capacity as lawgiver, and in virtue of which you laid down the laws of the ideal Polis'.[1] This condition it is the end of the 'second education' to fulfil.

There are two senses, a maximizing and a minimizing one, in which this condition might be understood. It might mean that a class or body within the city must undertake the whole task of city-founding, or Nomothesia, hitherto performed by Glaucon; i.e. that it must not merely understand but itself create the constitution within which its function of ruling is to be exercised. Unless it means at least this, the reality of the city will not be secured. It might mean, on the other hand, no more than that the rulers must possess an insight into the principles upon which Glaucon constructed the constitution in order to preserve it hence-

[1] vi. 497c, d.

OBJECTS OF POLITICAL PHILOSOPHY

forth; i.e. that even after the 'second education' the rulers are confined to the function of preserving what is already laid down.[1] It is important to observe that even on this minimizing interpretation the condition demands in the rulers a kind of activity no longer analogous to a Techne, since it presupposes in the ruling class a knowledge of the form of which it itself is the matter; but it does not now achieve the end for which it was inserted, namely to secure the reality of the city. Only the maintenance, not the construction, of the constitution is now taken out of the hands of Glaucon; and so long as the constitution owes its being only to his philosophical speculations it is condemned to the unreality of a Utopia, while its inhabitants can be no more than creatures of thought.

There is no doubt which of these interpretations is more properly to be termed the Platonic. In spite of some wavering in his thought and confusion in his language,[2] Plato surrenders the idea that his rulers can do more than preserve a constitution already founded, and accepts the consequence that his Polis cannot be real. We may indicate first in the briefest possible outline to what conclusions that condition might have led if taken in its fuller meaning, and will end this chapter by considering how far Plato's own doctrine represents a genuine step towards them.

The governors, endowed with the power of constitution-making, would be no longer a ruling class, but a sovereign body. By this single stroke the Polis would have become a State.

A State is differentiated finally and conclusively from any

---

[1] In other words, that their function is still confined to φυλακή, not extended to νομοθεσία. Cf. Appendix B, p. 37 *inf*.
[2] Cf. Appendix B, p. 37 *inf*.

natural object by embodying a sovereign will within it. I have used the word 'spiritual' hitherto in a negative sense, to mean simply that a state possesses characteristics other than those possessed by a natural object. It may be possible now to define two of these characteristics positively. That is, spiritual of which the essence involves the existence, and of which the essence is (not specific, but) individual.

(i) The former characteristic is that ascribed in the Ontological Argument to God,[1] and unless we see how the State possesses it, we shall not understand the startling ascription of divine attributes to the State by the great political philosophers from Hobbes to Hegel.[2] To define a State as that association which contains within itself the power to lay down its own constitution, means that, except in so far as it is real, it does not even fulfil the idea of a State. This is the meaning of the doctrine, which recurs in one form or another in all philosophies of the State, that power belongs to its essence. When Hobbes, e.g., maintains that the right of the sovereign extends no further than its power, he is maintaining that the essence of sovereignty is not an idea to which particular realization is accidental, but that the particular realization constitutes part of its essence. The State, to say the same thing in other words, is *causa sui*. On the Kantian dichotomy of the universe into a realm of nature and a realm of spirit, it must fall in virtue of this criterion into the latter; and cannot therefore be the object of a science of natural law and causal determination.

(ii) That the essence of a State is individual follows directly from what has just been said. Of a natural object (according to Greek doctrine, of all objects) the essence is

---

[1] And in Descartes' 'Cogito' argument to the self.
[2] Hobbes: 'That great Leviathan, that Mortall God.' Rousseau: 'The voice of the people is the voice of God.' Hegel: The State 'der irdische Gott'.

OBJECTS OF POLITICAL PHILOSOPHY 27

specific, i.e. it consists in the form common to all members of the kind, but what is peculiar to this particular is accidental. Therefore it is extraneous to the essence of such an object whether it is realized as a particular or not. But once grant it to be part of the essence that it should be realized, and the individual, without which realization is impossible, must itself be included in the essence.

The important conclusion follows from this that there can be no philosophy of the state in the method essayed by Plato in the *Republic*. This method is that of isolating the essential characteristics of the Polis from the historical accidents of this or that particular embodiment, and thus involves the assumption that the essence is specific and that the individual is accidental. Once that assumption is traversed the method loses its *raison d'être*. It is after all a conclusion easily drawn that, if the rulers take over the whole function of Glaucon, Glaucon will have nothing left to do.

It was not to be expected that Plato should pursue this path to its conclusion. If he had done so, he would have overturned in the *Republic* the foundations upon which the *Republic* is based.[1] He would have anticipated in his own experience the process of two thousand years of philosophy. But he does advance a definite step in this direction, and it would be ruinous to the understanding of the *Republic* to neglect its importance. He does not assert that it belongs to the essence of the Polis to be realized, but he does to the end imply that to the Polis (as to no other idea whatever) an earthly realization would constitute an added perfection.

---

[1] The extravagant expressions of anxiety and reluctance which he places in the mouth of Socrates when the question of the reality of the Polis arises, indicate that he had a dim and uneasy apprehension of the crucial issues involved. v. 472a; cf. vi. 497d, 503a, b.

He does not maintain that the rulers are to take the work of constitution-making out of the hands of Glaucon, but he does demand that they shall possess such an insight into the principles of the threefold constitution as will enable them to preserve it once it has been constructed; i.e. that this class shall possess an insight into the form of which it is itself the matter. The original conceptions of ruling as a Techne and of the order of the city as a natural order are implicitly transcended in these doctrines, and we have now to consider how Plato succeeds in developing the latter without disowning the former.

The rulers possess an insight not only into the form which they impose upon their material (the principle of the division of labour), but into the form of which they are themselves the matter (the principle of the threefold division of classes). It is this latter insight which constitutes the superiority of the status of the ruling class over that of the producing class, so that the one can be called 'golden', the other only 'bronze'.[1] The rulers owe their superior excellence, that is to say, to that very element in their activity to which Techne supplies no analogy. If their function were restricted to the task which first necessitated their introduction, namely to the imposition of form upon the productive Technae, this superiority would be gone. It is the limitation of the craftsman's vision to the form which he has to impose upon his material, and his inability to apprehend the form of which his own technical activity is the material, which makes him dependent upon a class of rulers and condemns him to be for ever a subject. But if the activity of ruling were in its turn saddled with the same limitation, the rulers themselves would be in their turn eternally subjects, subjects, namely, to the lawgiver who prescribes their relations both to each other and to the governed; and submitted to

[1] iii. 415.

OBJECTS OF POLITICAL PHILOSOPHY 29

an order which they must accept without comprehending it. The ruling class is freed from this servitude in so far as its understanding is extended beyond the order which it has to impose on its subjects in the producing class (division of labour) to that which determines its own relation to the classes of the auxiliaries and producers (threefold division of the Polis). Plato is enabled to attribute this extended understanding to the rulers without explicitly revoking the whole analogy of a Techne by a confusion, which consists in the naïve identification of the two orders, the division of labour among the subjects, which would legitimately fall in the province of a Techne of ruling, and the threefold division of the Polis, which emphatically would not. Only this confusion[1] enables Plato to maintain that compromise in which the political doctrine of the *Republic* essentially consists, and by which the language appropriate to the Techne conception of ruling is uncritically extended to embrace a conception of ruling which is inconsistent with it.

This confusion determines the meaning of 'justice' (Dikaiosune). This term is applied first to the perfect harmony subsisting between the Technae in the 'first city', later to the threefold order embracing rulers and ruled, and subsequently with a perfect impartiality to either. Plato assumes without question that the specialization of the functions of ruling and of fighting (the basis of the threefold division) can be justified simply as a further application of the principle of division of labour already established in the construction of the 'first city';[2] and it never occurs to him to reflect that, if the formation of these special classes were really no more than a further application of the original principle, it could never give rise to a *threefold*

---

[1] For evidence see Appendix A, p. 36 *inf*.
[2] Cf. pp. 9, 12 *sup*.; and ii. 374*a*; iii. 397*d, e*.

division of the Polis at all. It would merely add 2 to whatever had chanced to be the previous number of Technae; where there had been 5 there would now be 7, and where there had been 100 there would now be 102.[1] The introduction of the threefold division characteristic of the ideal Polis implies that the two classes of rulers and fighters are based on a principle so different from that of the division of labour that the whole multiplicity of Technae to which the division of labour gives rise may be regarded as forming a single class by contrast with these two.

A political society is first constituted by the supervention of the threefold form upon the division of labour,[2] and a clear recognition of what this supervention entails necessitates the consequence that the Polis can be included in neither of the two categories of the artificial and the natural. Since Plato is not in possession of a third category beyond these two, he is driven back upon the inconsistent compromise of maintaining that the Polis is both artifical and natural. It is artificial in so much as it is the product of the Techne of ruling and is in consequence dependent for its realization upon a precedent knowledge of its form. But it is natural in so much as the form now realized by the ruler's art had not to wait upon his art for its first realization, but only for its restoration; it is like the cured invalid, who is not therefore to be called an artificial product because his cure was wrought by a doctor's skill. Nor does this analogy

[1] The multiplication of Technae caused by the growing complexity of the city's wants and the introduction of 'luxury trades' to satisfy them, which is the mark of the city's transition from the condition of primitive health to the fevered state (ii. 373), is a genuine application of the original principle of the division of labour. But no rigour in the application of *this same principle* can lead to more than an increasing complexity of the organization of wants and supply.

[2] It does not, of course, displace the latter, which must still be maintained within the ideal Polis in the internal organization of the third or bronze class.

OBJECTS OF POLITICAL PHILOSOPHY

exhaust the differences by which the Polis is removed from the status of an artificial product. An artifact does not itself include the art by which it is produced, but the Polis includes its own artificers within itself; so that it must be compared in this respect not to the patient, but to the physician who cures himself. The acceptance of this latter analogy might seem to lead to the conclusion that the Polis is natural and not artificial at all; and this conclusion is in fact drawn by Aristotle. According to him an artificial object would be natural if it included within itself the art by which it is produced, and he expressly cites the instance of the self-cured physician to illustrate his conception of a natural object.[1] But this identification is possible only because Aristotle ignores the crucial distinction that, whereas natural health, or health naturally recovered, does not depend upon knowledge as a condition of its realization, the restored health of the self-cured physician does so depend. Plato, we may imagine, would have accepted the comparison of the Polis to the self-cured physician, but his recognition of what is involved in the doctrine that ruling is a Techne would have saved him from drawing from this analogy the inference that the Polis is merely natural.

But a recognition that the two orders which he identifies are in reality distinct would have prevented Plato from accepting this analogy at all. The order which it is the business of the rulers to realize (namely the threefold form) is not the same as the order which existed naturally in the primitive community. It is indeed an order which could not be realized naturally, because, except by including the class whose business it is to impose it, it would not be the (threefold) order that it is. The same peculiarity forbids to attribute its realization to a Techne. A Techne presupposes the precedent understanding of a form which receives from

[1] *Phys.* ii. 8 *ad fin.*

the 'technical' activity a material embodiment, but no alteration of its formal character. But the threefold form of the city cannot be conceived apart from the activity by which it is realized and from the matter in which it is embodied, because if these are abstracted, it loses that very character by which it is differentiated formally from the order of the 'first city'.

Thus it is only in virtue of his confusion of the two orders that Plato is able to regard the constitution of the ideal Polis (as the health of the self-cured physician may be regarded) as a product of the co-operation of art with nature. The resolution of this confusion would have entailed the consequence that the Polis is a product neither of art nor of nature nor of a combination of the two.

Even such a vague and inadequate hint of the consequences involved in a resolution of what I have called Plato's confusion should suffice to warn us that this is not a confusion in the ordinary sense; it is not merely a lapse which Plato himself might have corrected if it had been brought to his notice. It is the essence of Plato's whole political philosophy to hold together opposites which are not recognized to be opposed only because they are not realized to be distinct; to extend the function of the ruler beyond the limits of the 'technical' *without* surrendering the conception of ruling as a Techne; to include within Dikaiosune a spiritual content and yet to define it still as a natural order.

To distinguish, as we have distinguished, the division of labour from the threefold order of classes is thus, though it is a logical and necessary development of Plato's own premisses, not simply to correct Plato, but to disrupt him. It is to distinguish two different conceptions which he included under the single term Dikaiosune, and neither of the two conceptions which together take its place will be the

OBJECTS OF POLITICAL PHILOSOPHY

equivalent of that unique and untranslatable term. The distinction involved is that between the economic and the political order of human society.

It is only when this distinction has become explicit that the economic order can be recognized to be natural in a sense in which the political order is not, and the political order therefore conceived in opposition to the natural. This recognition finds expression in modern political philosophy at first in the opposition of the Natural to the Civil State, later (as a consequence of the Lockian principle that 'the obligations of the law of Nature cease not in society')[1] in the distinction of Society from State.

It is not, of course, true either that economic laws were the only laws held to govern the state of nature, or that the society later distinguished from the State was identified exclusively with economic society. Another kind of law also was called 'natural', namely that to which man owed obedience in virtue of his rational nature, as the economic laws were those to which his conduct was subject in virtue of his appetitive nature; and society, conceived in distinction from the state, was held to exhibit an order determined not only by economic laws, but also by those universal rules for the safeguarding of person, property, and contract which were deduced metaphysically from the reasonable nature of man, but derived historically from the system of Roman Law.[2] But economic laws are natural at least in one of the senses in which that term is opposed to positive, and an economic order constitutes a society at least in one of the senses in which society is opposed to State; so that the half, even if not the whole, of these later distinctions may be developed from the germ latent in the *Republic*.

When the distinction between Society and State had

---
[1] *Second Treatise on Civil Government*, § 135.
[2] See further, Ch. V, p. 145 *inf.*

been drawn, a discrimination became possible in the application of terms which Plato had applied indiscriminately. The term 'natural' was confined to the order of 'society', in contrast to the positive law which constitutes a State; and although the word had a twofold, indeed an equivocal, significance, according as 'society' was conceived to be constituted by one or other or both of those two orders which we may distinguish as the economic and the civil, both these orders have this in common that they must be contrasted with the order of the State as being universal whereas that is individual. By this distinction the word 'justice' first attained its modern, as distinct from its Platonic, connotation, meaning conformity to those universal laws of right which are prior to the state. By this distinction also what had been for Plato the single science of political philosophy fell into three distinct disciplines. Of the universal orders of society the one, the economic, became the object of Political Economy, the other of that *a priori* study of natural law, of which Locke's doctrine of property is an example and Kant's doctrine of the moral law a development. The former of these disciplines may be distinguished from the latter, as a science, according to a common usage of the term, is distinguished from a philosophy. But both alike agreed in having universal law as their object and in being thus opposed to the study of the positive law of the state which, being a study of the individual, must be neither scientific nor philosophical but historical.

Almost every confusion in which Plato is involved may be reduced to a failure to distinguish universal from individual. Thus he identifies beauty with usefulness,[1] and fails to distinguish the fine from the useful arts, because he does not see that beauty depends upon perfection of individual form, but usefulness upon perfection of specific

[1] τὸ μὲν ὠφέλιμον καλόν, τὸ δὲ βλαβερὸν αἰσχρόν, v. 457b.

OBJECTS OF POLITICAL PHILOSOPHY 35

form; so that the perfection of a tool, for example, is unlike that of a statue in that it depends upon the realization of an essence common to all others of the same kind, not of something unique to itself as an individual. Thus, again, he confuses the work of eugenics with that of education because he does not see that the end of breeding is the production of a perfect specimen of a type, but that of education the production of an individual excellence. And it may even be suggested that the Platonic identification of philosophical knowledge (Episteme) with love of the object known depends upon his failure to recognize that while the proper object of philosophical knowledge is universal, the object of love is individual.

Plato's identification of the universal order of society with the political order of the state is an instance of the same confusion; upon which we will expatiate here no longer than to point out one consequence of it. War presents no problem for Plato because he regards it simply as the activity necessary to preserve the structure of society from dissolution.[1] It has its sufficient justification in the fact that it is necessary for the maintenance of that order without which man can neither live well nor live. Plato never reflects that the only war which has this justification is war for the constitution of the Polis against the forces of barbarism. If we suppose the 'first city' of the *Republic* to be invaded by another city of the same constitution with itself, what is at stake is not the maintenance of social order, since this is present equally in both, and it is not necessary to suppose that it would be destroyed or even diminished in the city which surrendered its independence to another. The organization of division of labour and exchange of commodities is not dependent upon autonomy. The invader is not attacking this universal order, nor the defender

[1] See p. 8 *sup.*

fighting to preserve it against disruption. What is at stake is not whether this order should be preserved or not, but something quite different, namely whether the office of preserving it shall be vested in this body of men or in that. If the preservation of independence is to be held a just cause of war, it cannot be justified upon the principle that the preservation of a social order is necessary to the well-being of man; it requires a further principle, which Plato is very far from recognizing, namely that it is an essential condition of the freedom of man that the order to which he is subject shall be imposed upon himself by himself.

Appendix A

PLATO'S CONFUSION OF THE THREEFOLD DIVISION OF THE POLIS WITH THE DIVISION OF LABOUR

PLATO appeals to the principle ἓν ἔργον ἕκαστος, whether he is grounding the division of labour or the tripartite division: e.g. iii. 397e: οὐκοῦν διὰ ταῦτα ἐν μόνῃ τῇ τοιαύτῃ πόλει τόν τε σκυτοτόμον σκυτοτόμον εὑρήσομεν καὶ οὐ κυβερνήτην πρὸς τῇ σκυτοτομίᾳ, καὶ τὸν γεωργὸν γεωργὸν καὶ οὐ δικαστὴν πρὸς τῇ γεωργίᾳ, καὶ τὸν πολεμικὸν πολεμικὸν καὶ οὐ χρηματιστὴν πρὸς τῇ πολεμικῇ, καὶ πάντας οὕτω; When he is making ἀνδρεία (ii. 374a) and σοφία (iv. 428b–d) the attributes each of a special class, i.e. when he is introducing the *threefold* division of the Polis, he appeals in justification to the principle upon which the 'first city' was constructed, i.e. to the principle of the division of labour (ὡμολογοῦμεν δέ που, εἰ μέμνησαι, ἀδύνατον ἕνα πολλὰς καλῶς ἐργάζεσθαι τέχνας, ii. 374a).

δικαιοσύνη is referred indifferently to the maintenance of the division of labour (cf. ii. 372a, iv. 433a, 434a), and to the maintenance of the tripartite division (434b, c, 435b) and the reference of σωφροσύνη wavers similarly.

Perhaps of single passages iv. 443b ff. is the most striking:

OBJECTS OF POLITICAL PHILOSOPHY 37

Τέλεον ἄρα ἡμῖν τὸ ἐνύπνιον ἀποτετέλεσται, ὃ ἔφαμεν ὑποπτεῦσαι ὡς εὐθὺς ἀρχόμενοι τῆς πόλεως οἰκίζειν κατὰ θεόν τινα εἰς ἀρχήν τε καὶ τύπον τινὰ τῆς δικαιοσύνης κινδυνεύομεν ἐμβεβηκέναι.

Παντάπασιν μὲν οὖν.

Τὸ δέ γε ἦν ἄρα, ὦ Γλαύκων—δι' ὃ καὶ ὠφελεῖ—εἴδωλόν τι τῆς δικαιοσύνης, τὸ τὸν μὲν σκυτοτομικὸν φύσει ὀρθῶς ἔχειν σκυτοτομεῖν καὶ ἄλλο μηδὲν πράττειν, τὸν δὲ τεκτονικὸν τεκταίνεσθαι, καὶ τἆλλα δὴ οὕτως.

Φαίνεται.

Τὸ δέ γε ἀληθές, τοιοῦτόν τι ἦν, ὡς ἔοικεν, ἡ δικαιοσύνη, ἀλλ' οὐ περὶ τὴν ἔξω πρᾶξιν τῶν αὑτοῦ, ἀλλὰ περὶ τὴν ἐντός, ὡς ἀληθῶς περὶ ἑαυτὸν καὶ τὰ ἑαυτοῦ, μὴ ἐάσαντα τἀλλότρια πράττειν ἕκαστον ἐν αὑτῷ μηδὲ πολυπραγμονεῖν πρὸς ἄλληλα τὰ ἐν τῇ ψυχῇ γένη, κτλ.

Here the order in the Polis which is declared to be the counterpart of justice in the soul is explicitly identified with the division of labour; but in strictness the only order in the Polis which is analogous to the division of the soul is the tripartite division into classes.

Appendix B

IS THE PRODUCT OF THE 'SECOND EDUCATION' TO BE νομοθέτης OR φύλαξ?

The 'first education' is an education of φύλακες, and their activity of guarding or 'holding fast' clearly presupposes the prior activity of a νομοθέτης, who shall establish what they have to guard. Thus we are told, e.g. that as a result of this education the city has in itself δύναμιν τοιαύτην ᾗ διὰ παντὸς σώσει τὴν περὶ τῶν δεινῶν δόξαν, ταὐτά τε αὐτὰ εἶναι καὶ τοιαῦτα, ἅ τε καὶ οἷα ὁ νομοθέτης παρήγγελλεν ἐν τῇ παιδείᾳ (iv. 429b, c). The logic of the argument demands, as we have seen, and many references suggest, that the aim of the second, or philosophic, education is to produce the νομοθέτης, presupposed in the first education, to take over the work of constitution-making performed hitherto by Socrates and Glaucon; vi. 497c, d (quoted

p. 24 *sup.*), 500*d*, 500*d*–501*c* (οἱ τῷ θείῳ παραδείγματι χρώμενοι ζωγράφοι, πολιτειῶν ζωγράφος), 502*c*, 502*e* (all that was previously said—in the first education—about the rulers, must be retracted and gone over again from the beginning: τὸ τῶν ἀρχόντων ὥσπερ ἐξ ἀρχῆς μετελθεῖν δεῖ), vii. 519*c* (οἰκίσται), 540*a, b* (those who have completed the second education must καὶ πόλιν καὶ ἰδιώτας καὶ ἑαυτοὺς κοσμεῖν . . . καὶ οὕτως ἄλλους ἀεὶ παιδεύσαντας τοιούτους . . .).

But other and more numerous passages imply that the point of view is unaltered, that the end of the second as of the first education is to produce φύλακες, only that it does it more adequately than the first. Thus in vi. 503*d* the second education is distinguished simply as ἡ ἀκριβεστάτη παιδεία, and the philosophers who are its products as οἱ ἀκριβέστατοι φύλακες (503*b*); in vi. 484*b* the training of a philosopher is immediately connected with his ability φυλάξαι νόμους τε καὶ ἐπιτηδεύματα πόλεων; cf. ibid., *c* (φύλακα ὀξὺ ὁρῶντα cf. 506*b*). In vi. 499*b* ff., 502*a*, it is assumed that the philosopher-king who is to establish the ideal constitution can be produced only ἐκ τύχης, or ἔκ τινος θείας ἐπιπνοίας—i.e. it is not the object of the 'second education' to produce him. In viii. 551*b* the analogy of the κυβερνήτης is introduced without any modification. In vii. 525*b*, 527*c*, 530*e*, 534*d*, 536*b, e*, 'we' or 'you' (i.e. Socrates and Glaucon) are still referred to as the supreme lawgivers and educators, who lay down the principles which the ruling class have only to preserve or to apply: though in 530*c* the significant qualification is added, ἐάν τι ἡμῶν ὡς νομοθετῶν ὄφελος ᾖ.

This last batch of references may serve to remind us of the futility of collecting any more. We have not to 'convict' Plato of self-contradiction by collection of evidence. The only important thing is to see the necessity by which Plato's original position was bound to demand a development which could only have been admitted by surrender of the original position. The assignment of sovereignty to the guardians, which is logically demanded, would have implied the abdication of Socrates and Glaucon, and the abandonment of that constitution of an ideal State, which is the main design of the *Republic*.

II

DIKAIOSUNE AND FREEDOM IN PLATO

THE doctrine that form is essence is perfectly exemplified in the 'first city'. This community is constituted a community solely by the fact that it embodies the form of the division of labour, and it is called 'just' or dikaios according to the exactitude of its conformity. The craftsman, again, or demiurge, who is a member of this city of craftsmen, is constituted a craftsman by nothing else than by a skill which is the form of his natural faculties; this is his virtue or Arete. Finally, the justice of the community and the virtue of its member are linked together in this 'first city' by the closest bond of reciprocal implication; it is the skill of the craftsman which constitutes him a member of the economic organization, it is his place in the economic organization which both necessitates and alone makes possible the development of his skill.

The political doctrine of the *Republic* rests on the assumption that all this is unchanged in the ideal Polis; that the essence of this also consists in the embodiment of a certain form, and that its perfection is to be 'just', or to embody it exactly; that the virtue of the citizen consists in Dikaiosune, or in the form imposed upon the 'parts' of his soul; and that there is so strict a connexion between the Dikaiosune of the Polis and that of the individual that the individual is constituted a member of the city by the justice of his soul, and conversely that his place in the political organization necessitates the development of this individual Dikaiosune.

In reality this assumption breaks down. The real difference between the 'first city' and the ideal Polis is that in the one form is present, in the other form is self-imposed. Thus while the essence of the one is constituted simply by its form, the essence of the other consists in something else, namely in the activity within the city (sc. of the ruling class) by which form is imposed upon the city itself. Similarly, while it is the essence of the craftsman simply that his faculties should be informed, it is the essence of the citizen of the ideal Polis not merely that his soul should be informed, but that an element within his soul (sc. the reasoning part) should possess the power of informing the soul itself. This difference can be expressed properly only by saying that the essence both of Polis and of soul is not in reality form at all, but spirit, and their virtue or perfection accordingly not Dikaiosune, but freedom. Plato, of course, could not either express it or conceive it thus. He could conceive the activity of imposing form only as itself another form, namely as the threefold form, whether of the city or of the soul. He covertly introduces this form as the characteristic which distinguishes both the ideal Polis (or political) from the 'first city' (or economic organization) and the citizen of the former from the member of the latter. Then, failing to recognize that this form is after all different from any realized in the 'first city' and treating its realization in the Polis as no more than a restoration of the form embodied naturally in the former, he extends the conception of Dikaiosune to cover not only the constitution of the 'first city' and the Arete of its members, to which it is genuinely adequate, but also the threefold constitution of the ideal Polis and the Arete of its members, to which it is not.

The doctrine of the 'threefold form' in city and soul thus represents at one and the same time a transcendence of the point of view (adequate to the 'first city') for which the essence of the city is form and the essence of the citizen to be a craftsman, and a refusal to recognize that this point

DIKAIOSUNE AND FREEDOM IN PLATO

of view is transcended; what differentiates political from economic association and moral from technical excellence is conceived only as *another* form, and the ruler in consequence as *another* craftsman. It is our task in this chapter to show how some of the most important doctrines of the *Republic* spring from this, the Platonic compromise as we may call it, and how, nevertheless, the implication, though not recognized, is continually breaking forth, that the essence of the city is more than form, that the virtue of the citizen is not merely justice but freedom, and that the ruler (and even the subject) is essentially more than a craftsman.

It will be convenient to divide this task into three sections, considering first the threefold form in the city, secondly the threefold form in the soul, and thirdly the relation between them.

I

The order of the 'first city' is the form by which the various Technae cohere in unity, and its unity is natural in the sense that it has not been constituted in virtue of being known and is in no way the product of conscious reasonable activity. The introduction of the threefold order in the transition to the ideal Polis is meaningless unless it means that to this Polis it is essential that the form realized should be realized in virtue of its conscious apprehension by a class within itself, namely by the rulers. But Plato's whole view of the status and functions of the ruling class is determined by his incurable tendency to limit their activity to the *re*-imposition of the form already realized in the 'first city'. We have already remarked that this limitation is characteristic of the doctrine of ruling as a Techne, and we have noticed both some of the difficulties arising from this conception, and the confusion by which alone it was possible to uphold it. We have to add this further consequence of the same doctrine, namely that there must be ascribed to the rulers an essential superiority of status over all other craftsmen, to which the organization of the 'first city' offered no parallel, and which seems even to a superficial glance manifestly incompatible with the ideal of justice.

If a city achieves Dikaiosune in proportion as it embodies its proper form, it follows that the perfection of a city is that this form should be present, not that it should be willed. This consequence is perfectly expressed in the analogy which Plato constantly draws between justice and health and between the ruler and the physician. The perfection of a healthy body is not that its health should be the object of conscious purpose. That is not health, but hypochondria, and the healthiest body is that whose health has never been made the object of thought. No doubt, once this primitive health has been lost, it can be *restored* only by the conscious purpose of the physician, who has a scientific insight into the principle which constitutes health. But health restored has at least no greater value than health unbroken; and even for its restoration there is required no insight into its principle *on the part of the patient*, but only submission, whether voluntary, enforced, or cajoled, to the decrees of the physician.

It follows, since the form or order of the city is essential and the means by which it is attained only of secondary importance, that the order need not commend itself to the private judgement of the subject. It would be, as we have seen, no derogation from the ideal of Dikaiosune if the order of the Polis commanded the free assent of no single individual within it; if it were, as it is in the 'first city' an order not consciously approved but unconsciously obeyed, an order not so much accepted as rather not rejected. To restore this order, once it has been disturbed, does indeed

DIKAIOSUNE AND FREEDOM IN PLATO

require the approbation of the private judgement. Those who are to restore it, the rulers, must first have understood the ground of its necessity, and their work must be informed by a conscious acceptance of the principle which it realizes. But even then, even in the restored Polis, this approbation is not universally necessary; it is not necessary that it should be present in the subjects. It is the submission of the subject which is important, the ground of his submission is indifferent. It is not necessary that the order to which he submits should be approved by his private judgement, but only that he should surrender the right of private judgement.

Government, in a word, that is to say, the restoration and maintenance of justice, demands on the part of the ruler an insight into the grounds of the order he imposes, but it does not demand on the part of the subject an insight into the ground of the order he obeys.

This difference in the status of rulers and ruled is the key to the understanding of Plato's whole theory of government. The subjects have to conform, but not to consent, and therefore though the order of the Polis must be reasonable, it is not necessary that it should appeal to their reason. Thus censorship[1] and the medicinal lie[2] are proper instruments of government; and thus there can arise for Plato no problem of punishment, because coercion exercised upon a subject will have the same obvious justification as restraint imposed by a physician, that it is for his patient's good, not for his own.[3] Restraint so imposed is not punish-

[1] ii. 376b ff.   [2] ii. 381c, d.
[3] The standard is not, of course, Utilitarian; the right régime is that which will do the patient good, not that which the patient will most enjoy, nor is a state of health desirable as a means to pleasure or the avoidance of pain. But neither, on the other hand, is the standard a law of right which is quite indifferent to pleasure; to do good to a patient is to render him a perfect specimen of his type, and this will in fact mean that his capacities for pleasure receive the fullest satisfaction of which they are capable (ix. 486d–587a).

ment at all; it is merely a way of governing, an application of one of the two great instruments of pain and pleasure by which the ruler performs his task of imposing and maintaining order. Punishment can be distinguished from government only when some other condition is required for its infliction than the capacity of the subject to be improved by it. It becomes a problem only when it is assumed that the subject, unlike the patient or the child, must have consented to the order which claims his submission, because then the question arises: How can the consent of the subject justify the governor in overriding his consent?[1]

Plato does not always conceive the relation of ruler to subject on the analogy of that of the craftsman to his material, nor even on that of the physician to the animate material, his patient. He thinks of it perhaps even more often as a relation between educator and pupil. Rule and education, Arche and Paideia, are for him two names for the same thing,[2] and the life of a subject in the city is coextensive with the period of his education.

There are, in fact, important differences between the relation of craftsman to subject-matter, and that of master to pupil. Plato employs the two analogies without distinction, only because he does not recognize that the rulers do not stand in an identical relation towards each of the two classes inferior to them. The Auxiliaries are their pupils, the Third Class their subject-matter. But the

[1] It is almost superfluous to point out how closely the practice of Greek cities corresponded with Plato's theory in this matter. There was no distinction (or a very rudimentary one) between judicature and government. They had no capital punishment—the only punishment which can never be an instrument of discipline; and their law operated no less through reward than through punishment. These things are characteristic of the treatment reserved in the modern state for animals, idiots, and children.

[2] For illustrations see Appendix C, pp. 70 ff.

DIKAIOSUNE AND FREEDOM IN PLATO 45

differences of these relations, important as they are, do not affect the point which we are concerned to make here. The relation of master to pupil implies, no less than that of craftsman to material, a subjection of the latter to the former; and for the same reason, namely that the master has, and the pupil lacks, a knowledge of what the pupil has it in him to become. The pain inflicted on a pupil is no more judicial punishment than that inflicted on a patient; nor is the assent of his private judgement any more the condition of its justice.

Even the characteristic of education, that its end is the emancipation of the pupil, is irrelevant owing to the very significant fact that this emancipation coincides in Plato's city with his release from political subordination. If the pupil, having attained the use of reason, became an adult and responsible *subject* of the state, then indeed Plato would have been faced with the problem of justifying a relation of political subjection between men essentially equal. But since emancipation from the *status pupillaris* qualifies a man to become not a subject, but himself a ruler, this peculiarity in the relation of master to pupil does not entail any modification of the thory of government implied in the comparison of ruling with a Techne: the theory, namely, that political subordination is justified by the essential superiority of the ruler to the ruled.[1]

Plato's theory of government is thus not shaken, but only the more confirmed if the ruler is made an educator instead of a craftsman. The deficiency of the Techne analogy, namely that it denies all *reflexive* operation to the activity of ruling, is not supplied but shared by the analogy

[1] This assumption was, of course, not peculiar to Plato, but a characteristic of Greek thought. Cf. Aristotle's doctrine that some men are born to rule and others to be ruled. It is the counterpart in theory of the practice of slavery.

of education. We found in the previous chapter that the logic of Plato's own argument demands the conclusion that ruling is more than a Techne in virtue of this reflexive character; and we have now to show how the drawing of this conclusion at once makes questionable the difference of status, which seemed to Plato so obvious, and shakes the whole foundation upon which his theory of government is based. Since the same arguments which necessitate that ruling is more than a Techne, necessitate also that it is more than education, what is said in the following paragraphs about the former conception of ruling may be extended, *mutatis mutandis*, also to the latter.

We found the conclusion to be unavoidable[1] that the governors should be endowed not merely with that insight which, *qua* demiurges, they must possess, into the form of their material, but with a further insight into the form of which they are themselves the material. But if the ruler can be thus freed from the limitations of the craftsman's outlook, why not the other demiurges? It was, as we saw, only this assumed limitation of the craftsman's insight which made the introduction of a ruling class necessary at all.[2] Now that one man, the ruler, has been found capable of transcending the limitations of his craft, there is no reason in principle why this same capacity should not be assumed in all. Once assume it, and the *class* of rulers becomes superfluous; the members of the Polis will revert once more to that equality with one another in which they stood in the 'first city', before the class of guardians was introduced. The liberation of the rulers themselves from the limitations implied in the analogy of a Techne demands that they should surrender their station of pre-eminence.

'The citizens will revert to the equality of the "first city".' But this is in reality no reversion. The equality

[1] Ch. I, p. 28 *sup.* [2] Ch. I, p. 21 *sup.*

of the 'first city' was an equality of ignorance; men were equal only because none had transcended the limitations of his craft. But the equality demanded is an equality of Sophia, in which all men equally shall have transcended them. What is demanded is the abolition not of the ruling class, but of the subject class, and the equal possession by all citizens of the same 'wisdom' which qualified the guardians to rule. Such a city would differ from the natural community, which is the 'first city', not only, as Plato's ideal Polis differs, by possessing within itself a class able to impose form upon the whole, but by being able itself as a whole to impose form upon itself; in virtue of which ability a community is called free.

Thus the introduction of the threefold form into the city involves a declension from the ideal of justice, but a progress towards the ideal of freedom.

II

The term freedom, like the term Dikaiosune, is applied in different senses to the society and to the member of it. Hobbes remarks of the free city of Luca that although it has written on its turrets in great characters the word LIBERTAS, 'yet no man can thence infer, that a particular man has more Libertie, or Immunitie from the service of the Commonwealth there, than in Constantinople', and the contrast between the freedom of the state and the freedom of the individual in it is analogous to that of which Plato is conscious between Dikaiosune in the Polis and Dikaiosune in the soul. We have now to pass to the latter.

The conception of Dikaiosune as the realization of the form of man is exemplified in its perfection in the member of the 'first city'. Man is regarded here as a natural species, and the Dikaiosune which he achieves here is the realization of the essence of humanity conceived as a natural species.

The genus of the species is animal, and its differentia is rational: the characteristic of this conception of man is thus that reason is regarded not as that which differentiates man *from* natural species, but as that which differentiates man *among* natural species. The essence of man will be realized when he fulfils his generic nature in and through his specific differentia. As he is animal by genus he will fulfil his generic nature in the supply of his animal wants and in the exercise of his natural faculties; but as he is reasonable by differentia, he will realize his true essence only in so far as he supplies these wants by the application of reason and exercises these faculties under the guidance of reason. Reason is displayed in the conscious adaptation of means to end. The activity of a rational creature is distinguished from that of any other animal in that it is determined by the precedent intellectual apprehension of the form or end to be realized; that is to say, it is the characteristic and typical activity of man to be a demiurge and to exercise a Techne.

The exercise of this activity involves the imposition of a form not only upon the material of his craft, but upon the natural faculties of the craftsman himself. He can impose form upon his material only in virtue of an acquired skill, and this skill is not the addition of another faculty to those which he has by nature: no training can add to the endowment of nature in this way: but is the 'information' or organization of the faculties he already possesses. The form is his essence, and the degree to which his faculties are informed is the measure of his virtue (Arete). This is what makes him 'a good carpenter' or 'shoemaker', or 'good at' whatever his craft may be. The product of his craft is his Ergon or work, what he is good for or at.

Thus the perfection of a man depends upon the possession of no particular natural faculty, but upon the form

DIKAIOSUNE AND FREEDOM IN PLATO

of his natural faculties. This may be illustrated by the analogy of a tool. Neither the hardness of the head nor the length of the handle constitutes the essence of a hammer (for a pestle may have a hard head and a mallet a long handle), but solely its suitability to the end of driving nails. This is the form which determines the quality of each part, without being the quality of any. This suitability is the Arete of a hammer and the driving of nails its Ergon, or work, in which its Arete is realized. In precisely the same way the skill of a man at a craft does not depend upon the hypertrophy of any single faculty, but is a harmony or organization of the faculties, such as is suitable to the best performance of his proper task. This organization of the faculties is his Arete and his Ergon is the performance of the task.

Plato's ideal of Dikaiosune as the form of the particular man is perfectly realized in the Arete of the craftsman member of the 'first city', but it breaks down when the attempt is made to conceive it as the form of the three elements later distinguished in the soul. In the soul as in the city the introduction of the threefold form represents a declension from the ideal of Dikaiosune, but a progress towards that of freedom. The former involves the conception that the essence of man is his specific form, and that his virtue depends solely upon the perfection with which, not at all upon the means by which, the form is realized in the individual. Thus it constitutes no defect of the virtue of a craftsman that the training by which his faculties received their information should have been directed by another's insight rather than by his own. In so far as he is a craftsman, his consciousness is intended exclusively upon the form which he has to impose upon his material, and his eye is never turned inwards to the form which is to be imposed upon his own powers. The perfection of the craftsman, again, consists in the realization of his specific essence, i.e. of that capacity for rational (in the sense of technical) activity which he has in common with all other members of the same craft. Everything individual is accidental to his essence, and its realization is no part of his perfection. But the ideal of freedom[1] involves the conception that the Arete of man is moral virtue, that is, a form not to be imposed upon the soul without a man's own conscious apprehension of it; and that the essence of a particular man is what is individual to himself, not what is common to his species, i.e. not in form at all.

When Plato introduces the threefold division into the soul he takes it for granted that Dikaiosune is to be conceived as the form of its three elements in precisely the same sense in which skill is the form of natural faculties. And yet this assumption, though it is never explicitly questioned, is inconsistent with the conclusions actually drawn from the doctrine of the threefold division. If this assumption were true, it would follow that none of the three parts considered in itself and simply as material of this form could possess an intrinsic superiority over any other, nor indeed any intrinsic value or 'virtue' at all; it would follow that the possession of Andreia or Sophia or the development of the appetitive element is accidental to the perfection of a man in precisely the same sense in which such particular natural gifts as strength of arm and keenness of sight are accidental to the perfection of a craftsman; not, of course, in the sense that any skill can be developed except upon the material of such gifts: a man cannot be a good ploughman without a certain strength of arm, nor a good watchmaker without a certain keenness of sight,

[1] Or, more correctly, *one* ideal of freedom, namely the Rationalist. See pp. 56 ff.; and cf. p. 61, n. 1.

DIKAIOSUNE AND FREEDOM IN PLATO 51

and a man both blind and paralysed could hardly be a good craftsman at all: but certainly in the sense that the special development of any one of these gifts is not in itself essential to a man's perfection as a craftsman; the watchmaker may attain to the highest perfection of a demiurge without the one, and the ploughman without the other. It is the form imposed upon the particular faculties, not the virtue of any faculty in itself, which constitutes his Arete as a demiurge.

But Plato is very far from thinking that the virtues of the particular parts of the soul are accidental in this way to the perfection of a man;[1] otherwise it would be impossible for him to regard the ruler or the fighter who excels the mere demiurge who remains a subject, not in the Dikaiosune of his soul, but in the virtues of special parts of it, as constituting a more excellent type of manhood than the latter, or to attach to the two educations[2] of the guardians, whose end is the reproduction of Andreia and Sophia respectively, a greater importance than to the training of any demiurge. It would be impossible for him, in a word, to regard wisdom and courage as virtues at all.

To call Dikaiosune the form of the three parts of the soul is to assume that Thumos and To Logistikon, the 'spirited' and the rational parts, are themselves not formed but, equally with the passions, particular and natural, and thus material capable of receiving form. If it should appear

[1] This is most obviously true of Andreia and Sophia, which are assumed to have a positive and intrinsic value; but it is true also of the third, or appetitive, element of the soul, which is more than accidental to the perfection of man in that it is positively hostile to it.

[2] The 'first education' is described between ii. 376e and iv. 445e; Book vii is devoted to the 'second'. I have omitted here any reference to that part of the 'first education' (the earlier part ii, 376e–iii. 404e) which is designed to produce primarily (not ἀνδρεία, but) σωφροσύνη, but I hope that what I say of σωφροσύνη elsewhere (see Appendix D, p. 99 *inf.*) may to some extent both repair and explain the omission.

that Thumos and To Logistikon are not natural but products of education (that is, of information) and are therefore themselves informed by the universal, then the Dikaiosune by which these three elements are supposed to be related in unity will be a conception no less vicious and no less otiose than that of a form uniting form with matter. The conception of such a form is vicious because it implies that form is itself only another particular, otiose because form is united to its matter not in virtue of another form, but in virtue of its own inherent nisus towards realization. It is true, of course, that neither To Logistikon nor To Thumoeides[1] *is* the form of the soul; but they can be differentiated from among the natural faculties only in so far as they are conceived the one as that within the soul which is active in knowing this form, the other that which is active in willing it. What imposes this form upon the passions, and thus constitutes the unity of the three parts of the soul, is not indeed the nisus of the form itself, but still less is it another form; it is nothing else than the activity of the subject in knowing and willing the form. The weakness is the same in Plato's doctrine of threefold form whether in the Polis or in the soul; namely that he had no resource of thought or language by which he could represent the activity of realizing form as anything other than itself a form.

We have to show in detail how Plato's doctrine of the threefold division of the soul does in fact imply that To Thumoeides and To Logistikon are themselves informed in a sense incompatible with the assumption that they are matter for information by Dikaiosune; and that this implication carries with it a new conception of the nature of man, according to which his proper virtue is to be not just but free.

[1] The 'spirited' element.

DIKAIOSUNE AND FREEDOM IN PLATO

It is significant that Thumos is not distinguished from the natural passions on its first introduction;[1] but it is not long before Plato is compelled to make the distinction[2] and even explicitly to revoke the initial assumption.[3] It soon becomes clear that its excellence, Andreia, is not attributable to an accident of birth, but is produced by an education directed by reason. It follows from this that it is not a *particular* passion, instinct, or desire, for neither education nor reason can usurp the function of nature and increase the faculties with which the human animal is naturally endowed. The proper object of reason, whether in its theoretical or, as here, in its practical employment, is form and not matter. As in science it knows form, so in education or in ruling it produces form, or *informs* in the one or the other respectively of the two senses of the word. It follows that Andreia, in so far as it is the product of education is not a high degree of passion, but a form of the passions; and that Thumos, of which Andreia is the excellence, is not a passion among the other passions, but is these passions informed.

The information of the passions constitutes the unity of an individual; 'spirited' action is thus action initiated by the whole self, and may involve the frustration of any particular passion or desire.[4] 'Spirit' is roused to resentment by a threat to the integrity of the self; not by what is painful but by what is harmful, not by a privation, but by an indignity. But, as always in Greek theory, the form which constitutes the essence of the individual subordinates it at the same time to a supra-individual system (as the essence of a natural object is that specific form which assigns it its place in the hierarchy of species), and the realization of the form *may* require not the preservation

[1] e.g. ii. 375a.   [2] iv. 430b.   [3] iv. 440e.
[4] As Plato illustrates, iv. 439e ff.

but the annihilation of any given individual. Thus the same Andreia which finds its normal expression in the assertion of the individual self, may find expression in the negation of it; and the supreme act of courage is to meet death.[1] If this sounds paradoxical, we may reflect that the ill-called 'instinct' of self-preservation in animals which is normally expressed in the struggle of the individual for life, may equally bring the individual to destroy itself when the perpetuation of the species requires it.

The behaviour of animals is not free, and if 'Thumos' were no more than the instinct of self-preservation, Andreia would not contain even the germ of the idea of freedom. A free act is initiated not by the self merely, but by the concept of self, whether in the form of the self-regard which impels a man to assert his interest, or of the self-respect which may impel him to surrender it and a brave man to sacrifice his life. To *translate* Plato's Thumos as 'self-respect' is to go too far; all the concepts of reflection—self-knowledge, self-government, self-realization—are foreign to Greek thought, and the Greek philosophers attain only here and there in moments of supreme insight to explicit recognition of them. It is the essence of Plato's conception of honour (honour is the end of spirited action) to lie midway between these two extremes and to be differentiated clearly from neither. When Plato's warrior rejects an unworthy impulse, that is certainly not merely the blind following of a natural 'instinct'; but neither is it identical, say, with the action of a French gentleman under the *ancien régime*, who is moved by a *conception* of what his honour demands; and when he lays down his life 'for the sake of the noble',[2] his end does not indeed stir in him quite unconsciously, as the demands of its species stir in

[1] Cf. iii. 386b.   [2] τοῦ καλοῦ ἕνεκα. The phrase is Aristotle's.

DIKAIOSUNE AND FREEDOM IN PLATO

the stickleback defending its young, but neither is it fully present to his consciousness as an end.

In that which distinguishes it from the merely animal, 'Thumos' contains the germ of an idea of free will. Plato did not develop it, because he was not fully conscious of the contrast between man and animal.[1] His conception of the guardian's virtue is developed throughout by reference to the contrast not of the animal, but of the slave. It is slavery which the brave man fears more than death.[2] It is the slave who is incapable either of laying down his own life or of asserting himself in it. Slavery need not involve the frustration of any single passion or desire; what it essentially frustrates is the unification of those desires into a self. No doubt the desires and passions of the slave receive an order and a discipline, in so far as they are directed upon an end prescribed by the master. No doubt if the master is just, this end is the right one, and the slave achieves by obedience the proper perfection of his nature. What constitutes his lack of Andreia is that he remains dependent upon external prescription for the right direction of his conduct and never assimilates the principle into his own soul. He never passes that stage which Aristotle regards as the term of ethical training, the stage, namely, at which the pupil ceases to do just acts at the dictation of another and is moved to do them spontaneously by a principle within himself. The exercise of such a principle, moving to just acts without eternal prescription, is the virtue of Andreia, and it is clear that it implies emancipation from prescription. A man can realize Andreia only in so far as he is his own master.

But to be his own master is to be free; the opposite of Doulos, slave, is Eleutheros, a free man. The mere fact that Andreia is opposed to slavery is a sufficient indication

[1] Cf. p. 47 *sup*. [2] iii. 387*b*.

that some concept of freedom is implicit in it,[1] however different from any of those which we associate most readily with the term. Certainly the Andreios is free neither in the sense of a modern Rationalist morality, that his conduct is determined by his knowledge that it is right, nor in the sense of a modern Empiricism, that it is undetermined by anything except his liking. To achieve anything like the former freedom he would have to possess a higher virtue than Andreia, namely Sophia; to achieve anything like the latter he would have to relinquish Andreia itself. Andreia is freedom in what we may call the Pagan sense of the word. It was the virtue of the free citizen of the autonomous city-state of Greece.

We may notice a negative characteristic of this conception of freedom. It lacks the reflexive significance of self-mastery introduced by Stoicism and adopted by Christianity. The Andreios, emancipated from submission to mastery, exercises mastery not upon himself, but himself in turn upon another, so that the realization of his freedom presupposes the institution of slavery, and he is not more necessary to the slave than the slave to him if either is to realize his end.

For this reason the Andreia of the guardians in Plato's Polis depends upon the existence of a class who have it not. Plato himself asserts that to be master of oneself is a nonsensical conception,[2] and draws the consequence that the soul has parts. The inequality of classes in his Polis is no less a consequence of the same denial.

The virtue peculiar to the highest class of guardians is Sophia, or wisdom. It is the excellence of To Logistikon,

---

[1] Cf. iii. 387b, '... παισὶ καὶ ἀνδράσιν οὓς δεῖ ἐλευθέρους εἶναι, δουλείαν θανάτου μᾶλλον πεφοβημένους, where ἐλεύθερος and ἀνδρεῖος are clearly interchangeable terms.   [2] οὐκοῦν τὸ μὲν κρείττω αὐτοῦ γελοῖον; iv. 430e.

DIKAIOSUNE AND FREEDOM IN PLATO

the element of the soul by which it is enabled to apprehend Logos, the principle of form or order.[1] Possession of it is thus indisputably necessary to those whose task it is to prescribe a law anew, or to restore the natural unwilled order, when that has once been lost. These acts of the guardians at least, acts of law-giving and not of obedience, fulfil that condition of freedom which Kant expressed when he declared that free acts are determined not in accordance with a law, but by the conception of a law. We have seen how nearly insuperable was Plato's reluctance to recognize that the function of the rulers must be more than the prescription of law *to others*, or that it is logically necessary that they should also give law to themselves. If he had recognized this, his rulers would have enjoyed freedom in Rousseau's sense of the word, in which 'obedience to a law which we prescribe to ourselves is freedom'. If he had made intelligent insight into the principle of a law the pre-condition not only of prescribing a law but of obeying it, if, that is to say, he had made Sophia as well as Dikaiosune the universal virtue of all classes of the city, then freedom would have taken the place of justice as the ground and end of his political society, and the Platonic Polis would have been superseded by the Hegelian State.[2]

---

[1] Σοφία, like Andreia, is first introduced as the perfection of a natural faculty, analogous to that by which the watch-dog can recognize a member of his own family (ii. 375d–376e; cf. especially the significant concatenation ibid. φιλόσοφος δὴ καὶ θυμοειδὴς καὶ ταχὺς καὶ ἰσχυρὸς ἡμῖν τὴν φύσιν ἔσται ὁ μέλλων καλὸς κἀγαθὸς ἔσεσθαι φύλαξ πόλεως, as though these four attributes were all equally natural), but immediately outgrows this original connotation.

[2] There is a striking passage (vi. 468a, b) in which Plato actually does ascribe 'freedom' to the φιλόσοφος. The quality most alien to the philosopher's nature, he says, is ἀνελευθερία. This quality is identified with σμικρολογία, the attachment of the soul to objects of limited importance, and σοφία expels it by directing the soul upon the spectacle of 'all time and all being', in comparison with which the attractions of ὁ ἀνθρώπινος βίος fall back into their proper rank of relative insignificance.

The most important implication of Plato's doctrine of Sophia, and that in virtue of which it contained the possibility of these developments, is the following: the virtue of Sophia does not depend, as that of Dikaiosune does, upon the perfection with which form is realized in a subject, but upon the activity by which the realization is brought about. The spring of this activity lies not in the form, but in the substance which is to be informed, not in the (threefold) form which is to be imposed upon the soul, but in part of the 'matter' of the soul upon which this form is to be imposed; not in Logos but in To Logistikon.[1] This involves the consequence that the soul is of a nature entirely different from that either of any natural substance or of any product of art, seeing that its 'matter' is not the passive recipient of form, but the source of the activity by which form is realized, and its particularity therefore not accidental but essential to its perfection. It belongs to the following chapter to develop this consequence more fully, and I will only add here that it leads Plato himself to a doctrine of the essence of man radically different from that which he started by assuming, so that he comes to speak of To Logistikon not merely as essential to man, but as his whole essence.[2] This

---

Here again ἐλευθερία is used in a curiously limited sense; but the conception clearly anticipates the freedom which the Christian ascetic strove to attain by renunciation of the world.

[1] Logos and To Logistikon may each be translated 'reason', but the former is 'reason' in the sense in which it is an abstract noun, the latter is 'reason' in the sense in which it can be the subject of an active verb. To Logistikon is not, like Logos, a *potency*, but a *power* of realizing truth; not a δύναμις but a δυνάμενον; or, as Leibniz says somewhere of the monad, not a 'pouvoir' but a 'puissance'. On the importance of this difference cf. further Ch. III.

[2] In Book. ix τὸ λογιστικόν is called τὸ θεῖον ἐν ἡμῖν (589*d*; cf. ibid. *e*, 590*d*); it is also called τοῦ ἀνθρώπου ὁ ἐντὸς ἄνθρωπος (589*b*) which suggests the conclusion that it is the essence of man. ('The conclusion is made explicit by Aristotle: δόξειε δ' ἂν καὶ εἶναι ἕκαστος τοῦτο [sc. τὸ κράτιστον τῶν ἐν αὐτῷ], εἴπερ τὸ κύριον καὶ ἄμεινον. *Eth. Nic.* x. 1178*a*.)

DIKAIOSUNE AND FREEDOM IN PLATO

means that the essence of man is no longer specific but individual, and his perfection no longer to be substance of a form but to be subject of an activity; and thus Plato anticipates Descartes, who first made this conclusion explicit to thought, though it had been contained in the Christian religion as perhaps its most fundamental principle.

One further consequence of the tripartite organization must not be ignored. It results, as we have seen, in the exclusive attribution of two essential human excellences, Sophia and Andreia, to the guardian classes, and hence in a necessary inequality between guardians and producers. But the inequality is not wholly one-sided. If the ruling and fighting classes are the exclusive bearers each of one essential element of the soul, so also is the producing class. In it alone the element of desire, the third element of the soul, receives its proper and natural satisfaction,[1] namely in the activity of money-making.[2]

It is Plato's initial doctrine that Chrematistike is itself a Techne,[3] and its specialization in a single class therefore no more than an application of that division of labour which is a condition of any human excellence. If this doctrine could be upheld, then the ruler would not be the less a man for being excluded from it; any more than the shoemaker is the worse craftsman for not being a carpenter. But it can no more be upheld than the analogous doctrines that ruling and fighting are Technae, and the introduction of the threefold form signalizes the break-down of all three alike. The third class in the city is constituted by a

A very different doctrine of man is involved in saying that his essence is the divine in him, from that involved in saying that his essence is to be a rational animal.

[1] τὸ ἐπιθυμητικόν is χρημάτων φύσει ἀπληστότατον. iv. 442a.
[2] χρηματιστική. [3] i. 345b ff.

multiplicity of Technae; if Chrematistike were genuinely a Techne, it would be merely an additional one among them, and there would be nothing to constitute the productive Technae a single *class* at all. Plato is therefore forced to conceive Chrematistike as the distinguishing mark of the third class as such,[1] that is to say, as a common characteristic of all productive Technae. It is the expression of an appetitive nature which a man possesses independently of his special craft, and which is not, therefore, to be realized as a particular Techne, but by each craftsman in and through his particular work. By being excluded from this activity therefore the guardian is not simply limited in the sense in which any craftsman is limited by specialization, namely that having adopted one productive craft, he must renounce the alternative possibilities of others; he is excluded from participation in any productive work at all. This exclusion of the guardian from the possibility of productive labour is falsely presented by Plato as a case of the specialization of labour;[2] and the divorce of the Techne of ruling from Chrematistike is fallaciously supported by the analogy of other crafts.[3] The artisan satisfies the desirous, or 'epithumetic', element of his soul by devotion to a particular craft, and surrenders only the alternative possibilities of satisfying it by other crafts; the ruler renounces all satisfaction whatever of the entire 'third part' of the soul.

By this renunciation the guardians are deprived, both as a class and as individuals, of an excellence which the artisans possess. As a class they lack the differentiated organization, based on the division of labour, which is the

---

[1] iv. 434*b, c*. To be χρηματιστὴς φύσει disqualifies a man, therefore, for membership of the guardian class; iv. 433*a, b*, cf. iii. 415*e*, and even i. 346*c*.   [2] iii. 397*e*.
[3] Ibid. (οὐ χρηματιστὴν πρὸς τῇ πολεμικῇ).

DIKAIOSUNE AND FREEDOM IN PLATO

condition of the exchange of goods and of the pursuit of wealth, and which we must suppose to characterize both the 'first city' and the third class with the Polis. As individuals they are deficient in the element of desire, which Plato ranks third among the essential elements of the soul. It is not only the artisans who fall short of human perfection in being shut out from the possibilities of Andreia and Sophia. The guardians are maimed men also. In lacking desire they lack the capacity either to enjoy or to produce.

We have seen that either of the two higher faculties of the soul, the spirited or the reasonable, if allowed, as it is allowed in the guardians, to develop its own virtue, realizes a value other than justice, something which may be termed freedom in one or other of the senses of that most difficult term. The same is true of the desirous element. Simply to satisfy desire, without any regard to the reasonable order, which is justice, is a form of freedom, call it 'arbitrary', 'false', or 'negative' freedom if you please, but still indubitably freedom.[1] Plato himself calls it 'Eleutheria',[2] but his attitude towards it is curiously different from his attitude to the virtues of Andreia and Sophia, which we found to be, and to be recognized by Plato to be, themselves kinds of freedom. He regards this Eleutheria as so utterly

---

[1] Freedom was confined to this sense of the word in the Empiricist tradition of modern philosophy. 'A Free man is he that in those things, which by his strength and wit he is able to do, is not hindered to doe what he has a will to.' Hobbes. The Rationalists, on the other hand, (Kant e.g.) confined freedom to moral action, i.e. to action governed by conscious apprehension of reason. The germ of each conception is present in Plato, of the former in the ἐλευθερία of the χρηματιστής, of the latter in the σοφία of the ruler.

[2] See the whole description of Democracy and the 'democratic man' in viii. 555b–565e, especially 557b: ἐλευθερίας ἡ πόλις μεστὴ καὶ παρρησίας γίγνεται, καὶ ἐξουσία ἐν αὐτῇ ποιεῖν ὅτι τις βούλεται; 562b and c (ἐλευθερία is the end of Democracy). ἐλευθερία is conceived here, too, in conscious opposition to δουλεία (see 563d), and the last excess of democratic freedom is the emancipation of slaves (563b).

subversive of just order that the very establishment of a Polis depends upon its repression.

The freedom of Sophia and the freedom of Andreia were really themselves inconsistent with the ideal of justice. To call them virtues was to attribute to the activities of two parts of the soul an intrinsic value beyond that of the balance between the parts. In the face of this inconsistency Plato chooses rather to sacrifice his original ideal of justice than his nascent ideal of freedom. So far from demanding that these freedoms shall be stamped out in the Polis, he comes to see it as the essence of the Polis that it shall provide a framework within which these freedoms shall be nourished and exercised; for it is after all nothing but the presence of these freedoms within it which distinguishes the ideal Polis from the brutish condition of the 'first city'. It is as though Plato felt that these two freedoms somehow included and surpassed justice, while the freedom of desire was simply hostile to it; that those transcended, while this merely undermined it. The distinction between these two kinds of freedom will be found to be of primary importance for the understanding and criticism of Hegel.

Hegel will be found to repeat again and again as his fundamental criticism of the Platonic political philosophy that Plato's Polis was based on the suppression of this element of the soul, which therefore when it could be suppressed no longer burst out in manifestations hostile to lawful order and eventually destructive to it; and to contrast with this defect the might of the modern state, which can afford to tolerate this freedom within itself and even draws vitality to itself from its exercise. But this very criticism of the *Republic* is implicit in the *Republic* itself. The exclusion of this third Eleutheria from the Polis appears necessary so long as the Polis is tacitly identified with the

DIKAIOSUNE AND FREEDOM IN PLATO

ruling class within it, because freedom of desire is both inconsistent with the excellence of a ruler and incompatible with the performance of his task of preserving order. Plato never quite escapes from the confusion upon which this identification rests;[1] but if he had done so, if he had clearly recognized what the plan of his Polis implies, that the class of subjects who are not rulers is an integral part of the city, he must have seen that it was essential to his city also to allow some scope to freedom of desire. What is forbidden in the ruler is indispensable in the subject, since without it there would be neither the economic activity, by which the wants of the whole city are supplied, nor the economic organization by division of labour, which, though it is confined to the subject class, is still the substructure upon which the constitution of the entire Polis is erected.

III

Fully conscious though Plato is that Dikaiosune in the Polis and Dikaiosune in the soul are different things, and though his argument is almost everywhere devoted to showing that these two orders are analogous rather than that they are mutually dependent, it is the unquestioned assumption of the *Republic* that the achievement of the one Dikaiosune will imply the achievement of the other, and that submission to the Nomos of a well-balanced Polis will produce that balance of elements within the soul which is the perfection of the individual man.[2] This assumption is justified whether we consider the 'first city' or the ideal Polis. So long as the essence of the city is the economic order of want and supply, and the Arete of each member

[1] The exclusion of a class of slaves from citizenship in Greece implies a similar inability in the ordinary Greek to conceive that the city is constituted by anything but the class of masters.
[2] Cf. iv. 443c ff.

is his skill, or 'what he is good for', there is a perfect nexus of reciprocal implication between them. An economic organization can be based only on the specialized activities of skilled craftsmen; and conversely skill demands for its development a specialization which is possible only in an organized economic system.

This reciprocal implication between the Dikaiosune of the Polis and that of the individual still holds when the former comes to be identified no longer with the organization of Technae, but with the maintenance of the threefold form, and the latter no longer with the information of the natural faculties as skill, but with the balance of the soul's threefold constitution. The difference imported by this new identification is that the virtue neither of city nor of soul can be conceived any longer to be exhausted in Dikaiosune. The whole virtue of the craftsman is his skill, and of economic society its organization; that is to say, the essence of each is the form realized, while the matter in which it is realized, the natural faculties of the human animal and the trades of which economic society is composed, are accidental. But the three parts of the soul are not simply the matter of its threefold form as the natural faculties are matter for the development of skill, and the virtue of a man is not exhausted in his being just as the virtue of a craftsman is in his being skilful. Plato will not recognize this difference, and yet he implies it in the very admission that two parts of the soul have each a proper virtue, Sophia and Andreia, over and above the virtue of Dikaiosune, which consists in the balance of the parts. Nor are the classes of the tripartite Polis related as matter to the political constitution in the same way as the trades of the 'first city' to the economic organization. A class differs from a trade in the same way in which one of Plato's parts of the soul differs from a natural faculty, in being

DIKAIOSUNE AND FREEDOM IN PLATO

capable of a virtue of its own, and the city composed of classes differs from the economic society in the same way in which the soul of the man differs from the skill of the craftsman, in that its essence is not exhausted in the form of its parts, nor its virtue in the perfection of its organization.[1] Plato implies this difference whenever he implies that the tripartite Polis achieves an excellence beyond that of the 'first city'; but he is precluded from recognizing it by his failure even to distinguish the political constitution from the economic organization.

This is only an instance of the procedure which we have discovered to be characteristic of the whole *Republic*. Plato is introducing new ideas into a conceptual framework which will not hold them, and he is prevented both from developing the new and from discarding the old by his failure to perceive that they are not identical. This failure to discriminate, we must repeat, is essential to the whole of Plato's political philosophy, and to seek an enforced consistency either by excluding the new or by discarding the old would be to produce something which was either much less or much more than Platonism.

The conception of freedom is the new wine which bursts the old bottles. The philosopher in his wisdom, the soldier in his courage, and the producer in his money-making each realizes a perfection of a 'part of the soul' which is other than the balance among the parts. Each realization is freedom in a different sense, and each freedom is found to demand for its achievement not the satisfaction, but the sacrifice of the other parts of the soul. Thus wisdom can be perfectly achieved only in so far as the philosopher is released not only from the bondage of desire, but from all practical activity; and the reasoning part of the soul will attain the highest virtue of which it is capable when death

[1] Or, in that it is more than an organism.

has completed the task which the philosophical training began and has finally severed its attachment to the inferior parts of the soul.[1] Desire is clearly most free when it is free from all control by reason. Andreia above all, the virtue of the 'second part', is incompatible no less with the activity of reason than with the freedom of desire. It is achieved in the realization in conduct of a reasonable principle not apprehended by reason, but accepted on trust and by faith. This faith Plato calls Orthe Doxa, right belief, and he assumed it to differ only by defect from reasonable apprehension. But the alleged defect is what alone constitutes Andreia an ethical virtue, or virtue of character, at all. So long as the soldier, for instance, has only 'right belief' about what things are to be feared and what not,[2] his maintenance of this belief in the temptation of danger is an act of courage. But suppose understanding to have taken the place of belief, there can be no longer a temptation of danger, and the soldier will have realized indeed the intellectual virtue of wisdom, but he will have lost the opportunity of being brave. Andreia is the pagan freedom, it is the virtue by which a free man was distinguished from a slave. It was not entirely a false instinct which warned the opponents of Socrates that the indulgence of philosophical speculation was as destructive of the naïve virtue of the free-born citizen (καλὸς κἀγαθός) as his participation in servile pursuits for gain. Sophia is the anticipation of a new idea of freedom, the Christian, and the mutual contradiction of the two ideas is the reflection within philosophy of a conflict fought on a wider stage than that of any academy.

The several virtues of the parts of the soul are thus not

---

[1] In Book ix. 588 f. (cf. the myth of the monstrous beast) Plato clearly regards it as detrimental to the perfection of the highest part of the soul that it is bound by the necessities of 'this life' to the inferior parts.   [2] iv. 429e.

merely not included in the ideal of Dikaiosune as the tripartite balance, but are antagonistic to it; and although each demands a society for its exercise, this society is not the tripartite Polis, but the class. The philosopher must belong to a community of philosophers, the soldier to a comradeship in arms, the producer to an economic society; and thus each several part of the soul finds its objective counterpart in the organization of one of three *estates*. The organization of these estates is not only not included in the ideal of Dikaiosune in the Polis, but is positively hostile to it. Whereas that ideal implies the closest relation of reciprocal interdependence between each estate and the other two, it appears that each can best secure the freedom of its members by achieving the greatest possible independence of the other two. The community of philosophers can best achieve the freedom of its members by reducing to a minimum the ties which bind it to the world. The economic organization can attain its true development only when it is released from purposive control.

Each estate in being freed from its unity with the other two is freed from its local limitation. The first becomes a catholic brotherhood, the second a world-wide chivalry, and the third a system of private property, safeguarded by a universal code of law. None of these societies is any longer political; each is based upon a law which is, in one or other of the senses of the term, a *natural* law.

Dikaiosune, as the threefold form of the soul, is the link which unites its parts into a single personality: as the threefold form of the Polis, it is the bond which fuses the three classes into a political society. Plato is wrong in thinking that the Dikaiosune of the soul includes all human virtue, and wrong therefore in supposing that his political constitution supplies the framework for the realization of all human excellence. But his contention that the unification of parts within the individual soul and the unification of classes in an individual state are mutually dependent, is justified by the reflection that the disintegration of the one unity under the solvent influence of freedom carried with it the dissolution of the other. The dawn of the modern era, furthermore, is marked by the simultaneous renaissance of both ideals. As the perfection of the human soul is conceived once more to lie in the fusion of all its elements into an individual personality, so the perfection of human society comes to be placed once more in the unification of its classes into a national state.

The received dogma that there is a fundamental opposition between the individual and the state is true, or the exact contrary of the truth, according to the meaning which is attached to 'individual'. The phrase is generally used to include two different oppositions, that between the laws of the state and the individual's conscience, and that between the laws of the state and the individual's interest. Each of these is a genuine opposition. Conscience is that element of the soul which Plato named To Logistikon, and it seems to demand for its perfect freedom a law indeed, but a law transcending local limitation. The interest of the individual is the satisfaction of what Plato called the third element of his soul, and this implies his membership of a society in which economic motives have free play. The laws of such a society, whether we think of them as the system of rules for the maintenance of property, or as the laws exhibited by economic activity within such a system, are not, like the positive law of an individual state, subject to any territorial limitation.

In each of these cases the opposition of the individual to the state depends upon his membership of a universal society; but in each case his membership of this wide society engages one only of the 'parts of his soul' to the exclusion of the remainder. We can speak of them as oppositions between the individual and the state at all only so long as we are content to identify the individual with a single part of himself, but if we mean by 'individual' a personality in which all parts of the soul are united, not one developed to the exclusion of the rest, then the fusion of these universal societies into a national state is not antagonistic, but is the objective counterpart and necessary condition of such development of personality. There is a real opposition both of the societies against absorption in the state and of the 'parts of the soul' against absorption in the individual; and these are what is obscurely meant but confusedly expressed by 'the opposition of the individual and the state'.

A renaissance is not a simple recurrence, and it was not possible simply to re-establish the Greek ideal of Dikaiosune as the unity either of the soul or of the state. Dikaiosune was a unity excluding freedom; the modern conception both of personality and of state was of a unity based upon freedom.

This is the cardinal issue upon which the modern philosophy of the State differs from the ancient philosophy of the Polis, and upon which in particular Hegel's political philosophy not only differed, but was clearly recognized by himself to differ, from Plato's. Hegel is never weary of insisting that the modern state is based upon freedom and not, like Plato's, upon the exclusion of it. In order fully to understand this difference I have no doubt that it would be necessary to have understood the philosophy of the intervening period, and in particular to have seen how the ideas of freedom, germinal in Plato, were developed in the Christian philosophy of the Middle Ages. I do not, of course, propose to attempt any such task; I shall endeavour instead to approach the Hegelian philosophy of the State as it were by a short cut and a side entry by considering the criticisms of Plato's political philosophy by which Hegel elucidates his own. Great philosophers have not always been the best critics of their own predecessors or the best judges of their own distinctive importance; but we may attempt with Hegel a method which could hardly fail to be misleading with any other philosopher, because he was himself the first and is still the greatest of historians of philosophy.

Appendix C
EDUCATION AND GOVERNMENT IN PLATO

ἀρχή and παιδεία are interchangeable terms for Plato. Thus he speaks in ix. 590e of ἡ τῶν παίδων ἀρχή, τὸ μὴ ἐᾶν ἐλευθέρους εἶναι, ἕως ἂν ἐν αὐτοῖς ὥσπερ ἐν πόλει πολιτείαν καταστήσωμεν.... The latter part of the sentence might seem to imply that there is a term to the educational process, upon reaching which the pupil becomes a free and responsible subject of the Polis. But this is not so; the life of the subject in the Polis is coextensive with his pupillage. The term of the process is the point at which he is qualified to become not a free subject, but a ruler, i.e. himself in turn an educator.

The identification of ruling with educating may be illustrated further by x. 599d–600a, where Socrates is disputing Homer's claim to wisdom: Ὦ φίλε Ὅμηρε, εἴπερ μὴ τρίτος ἀπὸ τῆς ἀληθείας εἶ ἀρετῆς πέρι, εἰδώλου δημιουργός, ὃν δὴ μιμητὴν ὡρισάμεθα, ἀλλὰ καὶ δεύτερος, καὶ οἷός τε ἦσθα γιγνώσκειν ποῖα ἐπιτηδεύματα βελτίους ἢ χείρους ἀνθρώπους ποιεῖ ἰδίᾳ καὶ δημοσίᾳ, λέγε ἡμῖν τίς τῶν πόλεων διὰ σὲ βέλτιον ᾤκησεν...; σὲ δὲ τίς αἰτιᾶται πόλις νομοθέτην ἀγαθὸν γεγονέναι καὶ σφᾶς ὠφεληκέναι; Here the assumption is clear that the task of the lawgiver is to make men better, i.e. is the same as that of the educator (cf. 600c: παιδεύειν ἀνθρώπους καὶ βελτίους ἀπεργάζεσθαι); and a subsequent sentence is more striking still:

DIKAIOSUNE AND FREEDOM IN PLATO

ἀλλὰ δὴ εἰ μὴ δημοσίᾳ, ἰδίᾳ τισὶν ἡγεμὼν παιδείας αὐτὸς ζῶν λέγεται Ὅμηρος γενέσθαι; (600a). The alternative which we should express as that between being a statesman and being a teacher, presents itself to Plato simply as the alternative between educating 'publicly' and educating 'privately'.

Here, as elsewhere, Plato is reflecting the principles which underlay Greek practice in classical times. Private education was unimportant, but life in the city was the school of the citizen. Compare the answer given to the father who inquired how he could best educate his son: 'by making him citizen of a well-ruled city.'

III

HEGEL'S CRITICISM OF PLATO: THE 'SUBJECTIVE ELEMENT'

MODERN political theories differ from ancient principally in making freedom the ground, end, and limit of the state; however much modern theories may differ from one another, according to the variety of meanings which freedom may bear, these differences sink into a relative insignificance when they are seen to be differences only in the interpretation of a principle which all have in common and in virtue of which they may all be contrasted with the ancient theories that the state is natural.

Hegel fastens upon this difference whenever he seeks to develop his own theory by criticism of Plato, but he expresses it in a variety of phrases. The lack discernible in the Polis, and reflected in the political theory of the Polis, is its failure to respect the 'rights of the individual', the 'freedom of the individual', the 'right to satisfaction of the particularity of the subject'.[1] But the term perhaps commonest of all in Hegel's mouth in this connexion is 'subjectivity'; it is characteristic of the State, in contrast with the Polis, that it allows play to 'the subjective element',[2] and 'subjective freedom' is 'the principle of the modern world'. It is important, therefore, to understand the exact meaning of this term.

We shall do this most easily if we think of the original sense of the word 'subject', according to which it is the Latin translation of the Aristotelian ὑποκείμενον and means simply subject of predicates. According to the Aristotelian doctrine the essence of anything is exhausted in its predi-

---

[1] 'Des Subjekts': the word does not mean the political subject, or imply a contrast with the ruler.   [2] 'Das Subjektive.'

THE 'SUBJECTIVE ELEMENT'

cates, in those two predicates, namely, of genus and differentia, which together constitute the definition and declare the Form or Eidos of the thing. This Form or Eidos, like everything that can be predicated, is necessarily general; it is its nature to be capable of predication of other subjects than that to which it is in any given instance applied. Of course there is always in any particular subject a residual element which is not exhausted in any predicate or number of predicates. This element is, on the Aristotelian doctrine, material as opposed to formal, accidental as opposed to essential, passive as opposed to active, individual as opposed to general. It may be called with strict propriety the 'subjective element'.

The virtue which, according to Plato, constitutes the virtue of a man *qua* citizen is Dikaiosune, and, as formal, it is necessarily also general. It can be identical in any number of particular subjects, and the particularity of the subject in which it is realized is accidental to it; that is to say, the subjective element is excluded from its essence. In so far as it is regarded as the essence of a particular soul to be just, its essence is placed, like that of natural objects, in something to which the individuality of the particular subject is indifferent.

The subjective element is not excluded in the same way from the virtue of Sophia, which we found to be an anticipation of freedom in one of the modern senses of that word,[1] nor is it excluded from that activity of the 'appetitive part', which Plato condemns under the name of Eleutheria, and which corresponds to the second of the modern senses of freedom.[2] The following reflection may make this clear. Dikaiosune is the presence of Logos in the soul, it is the

---

[1] Ch. II, pp. 57 ff. *sup*.

[2] Ch. II, p. 61 *sup*. I reserve for a later treatment the part played by 'the subjective element' in Andreia; cf. pp. 91 ff. *inf*.

information of a given matter by a certain form. The form is the threefold relation of the parts of the soul, the matter is those parts considered apart from the relation, To Logistikon, To Thumoeides, To Epithumetikon. So far there is nothing to which the ordinary Greek doctrine is not applicable. The form is general and essential, while the subject, that material element designated by the neuter substantives, is individual and accidental. Above all, the activity to which the information is due must be attributed, so long as we adhere to this point of view, to the form and not to the matter, to the Logos and not to the subjective elements whether of To Logistikon, To Thumoeides, or To Epithumetikon.

But with Sophia the case is different. This activity also is an information of the subject by Logos, but it is an information in which the spring of activity lies not in the informing Logos, but in the subject to be informed, in that very 'subjective element' which is designated To Logistikon. That is to say, the subjective element, which is the individual element, is not accidental, it is not merely material capable of being informed, or a passive potency, but is an active power to realize form in itself and is thus not accidental but essential to the realization. The difference between Dikaiosune and Sophia is the difference between that information which is presence of form and that information which is knowledge of form. In the former it is the form which is active, while the subject is not more than the passive material upon which this activity is exercised; but in the latter it is the subject itself which is active, it *informs itself* by an activity of knowing, of which the form is no more than the passive object. This difference may be illustrated further by the different meanings of the English term 'to realize', as (1) 'to make real' and (2) 'to become conscious of'. Both Dikaiosune and Sophia may be termed 'realization of form', but each in a different sense. In the former the form is realized (made real) in the subject, and the spring of the activity of realization lies (whether or not in the form itself) at any rate outside the subject. In the latter, when the subject becomes conscious of the form, the form is realized not only in but by the subject, and the spring of this activity lies in the subject itself. The subject becomes thereby a subject in a further sense. It is no longer merely the subject in which predicates inhere (subject as opposed to predicate), but is subject of an activity (subject as opposed to object). Thus of Sophia not the form (the general) is the essence, but the appropriation of the form by the subject, the individual.

There is thus included in the Platonic virtue of Sophia what Hegel calls the 'element of subjectivity'.

But this virtue is not, according to Plato, proper to a man *qua* member or citizen of a Polis, but only *qua* ruler or guardian of it, and the 'subjective freedom' which it ensures is not coextensive with justice, since all members of the city are just equally, but with the activity of imposing or maintaining justice, which is reserved for the few. The only virtue open to those members of the city who are not guardians appears to be Dikaiosune,[1] and the subjective element in the soul of the citizen has no part in the realization of this virtue. The members of the subject class stand to the rulers in the relation of material to craftsman—a conclusion which is indeed no more than the converse of the doctrine that ruling is a Techne. Their souls are passive material for the reception of an active form, but are the source of no responsive activity.

If, then, we pay regard to the activity of the subjective element in the virtue of Sophia, it is clear that we cannot say that the scheme of the Platonic Polis is based upon the

[1] On Sophrosune see Appendix D, p. 99 *inf.*

entire exclusion of 'subjective freedom', since it essentially demands such freedom in the rulers. Hegel's criticism is true only in the limited, but still vitally important, sense, that the constitution of Plato's Polis implies the exclusion *of all who are not rulers* from participation in this freedom.

We have assumed so far that the 'subjective freedom' which Hegel asserted to be lacking in the Polis, is to be identified with the manifestation of it in Sophia. But this is not its only manifestation. The third part of the soul has an equal right with the first to the title of the 'subjective element', and the satisfaction of appetite in the economic activity of money-making or Chrematistike is also a kind of subjective freedom. Hegel's criticism of Plato takes on a different aspect if we understand the terms in this sense, identifying his 'subjective element' with Plato's 'third part' and his 'subjective freedom' with freedom to satisfy desire.

Plato's attitude to this subjective activity is quite different from his attitude to the subjective activity of reason; and indeed this activity is itself different in an important respect from the former. The activity of the subject in Sophia is directed upon a form or universal and is wholly determined by it, whereas desire is directed upon a particular object. It is therefore quite incompatible with that self-surrender to direction by the universal which is the essence of just rule for Plato. It is clear that Plato must exclude such an element from the souls of his rulers, just as he excludes all economic differentiation, which is the machinery of Chrematistike, from the organization of their class.

Is this element excluded by Plato also from the souls of the subject class? And is it true, therefore, that this freedom is entirely absent from the Platonic Polis?

It might seem that we must answer No, when we reflect that Plato allows us to infer both that the subject himself is

THE 'SUBJECTIVE ELEMENT' 77

'chrematistical by nature',[1] and that the organization of the subject class is based upon division of labour. But to answer simply No would be to ignore the significance of the fact that Plato does no more than allow us to infer these things. If he had himself recognized that the subject, even in the well-ordered Polis, achieves a satisfaction unknown to the ruler; and that the subject class develops in itself and in virtue of no Sophia an order different from the political order which it is the business of the ruler to impose by his Sophia: then he would indeed both have forestalled Hegel's criticism and have anticipated something of Hegel's own doctrine, but he would have done it only by an explicit abandonment of the theory of Dikaiosune which is presupposed both by his ethical and by his political philosophy.

The main ethical thesis of the *Republic* is that justice pays, or that the man whose soul is most completely ordered by reason is also necessarily the happiest man. The proof of this thesis depends upon the position that there is no positive element in the satisfaction of desire which is not wholly absorbed into the realization of good by reason.[2] The former satisfaction will differ from the latter only by defect and confusedness. It will be related to it as the sensuous perception of a particular (triangle, e.g.) is related[3] to the intellectual comprehension of the universal. As the former is the glimpse of a truth fully realized by the latter and contains no element of knowledge not included in the latter, so the satisfaction of desire is a fleeting foretaste of the reasonable good, but contains no element of happiness not included in the enjoyment of the good by reason. This ethical theory quite clearly involves the denial of the suggestion that the subject achieves a satisfaction not open to the ruler. If the satisfaction of reason includes the satisfaction

[1] χρηματιστὴς φύσει.
[2] ix. 586d–587a.
[3] I mean, of course, on Plato's theory of knowledge.

of all other parts of the soul, then the ruler realizes in himself all the happiness of which the soul of man is capable; and the subject will achieve such happiness as he is himself capable of *not* by the satisfaction of the appetitive element which is his distinctive characteristic, but by a subordination of appetite to reason precisely similar to that which takes place in the soul of the ruler himself, except that the subject, having no principle of reason in his own soul, must submit to be governed by that in the soul of the ruler.

The main political thesis of the *Republic* is that it is for the good of the subject class to be governed. The activity of the ruling class being the imposition of form, the thesis must hang from the assumption that it is the nature of the subject class to be wholly lacking in form, and thus to depend for its very being (because there is no being but is constituted by both matter and form) upon that which the ruling class has to supply. From this assumption, Plato's conclusion will follow, that the unity of the city is the closest of all unities, since its elements are bound together by a tie which is analogous to no physical relationship of individual things with one another but only to the metaphysical relation of matter to form within the constitution of an individual thing. This political doctrine is clearly inconsistent with the ascription to the third class of an order of its own, generated simply by its economic activities, and independent of the political order imposed by the rulers.[1]

[1] It may throw these two Platonic theses into a clearer light if we point out that they were contradicted in the ethical and political theory of English Empiricism. It was first asserted in the Empiricist Ethics that the gratification of the senses affords a positive satisfaction not accessible to reason, and not included in any realization of the good by reason; so that the immediate enjoyment of sensuous experience is not merely sufficient evidence for the judgement 'This is good', but is the only possible evidence.

This Empiricist doctrine of the autonomy of sense within the soul has its counterpart in the Empiricist doctrine of the autonomy of the

THE 'SUBJECTIVE ELEMENT'

Although, therefore, the inferences might (or rather must) be drawn from Plato, both that a subjective element of the soul finds in Chrematistike a satisfaction which is to be found neither in ruling nor in being ruled, and that the subject class within the state exhibits an order which is identical neither with the order of the guardian class nor with the political order by which class is united to class, Plato himself is prohibited from drawing them by the political and ethical doctrines of Dikaiosune which we have just summarized.[1] The doctrine of Dikaiosune justifies Hegel's criticism that Plato excludes this subjective freedom from the souls of the citizens, and any field for its exercise from the constitution of his state. And if it is true that Hegel is here only developing against Plato a doctrine which may be discovered to be implicit in Plato himself, the same may be said of any true criticism which one philosopher can make of another.

Hegel expresses his criticism of Plato simply by saying that the Platonic Polis allows no scope for 'subjective

economic sphere within society. The Empiricists discovered that the economic operations of man in society are not susceptible of political control; and further that, lacking this control, they do not remain unorganized and chaotic, are not simply material awaiting a form, but that they naturally and without conscious direction generate a law and order of their own. The laws of this economic sphere they then made the object of a science distinct from Political Philosophy, namely Political Economy; and thus first made possible the distinction between the economic and the political orders, which Plato had confused or identified. (Ch. I, p. 29 *sup.*)

It is hardly necessary to add that the early Empiricists were prone in their theories both of Ethics and of society to overlook the distinction between claiming autonomy and claiming autocracy for the 'third element', whether of the soul or of the state.

[1] And, we may remind ourselves, he is enabled to occupy an ambiguous position, in which they are neither drawn nor disavowed by his illicit identification of the division of labour with the threefold form and of Chrematistike with a τέχνη.

freedom' and can maintain itself only by suppression of the 'subjective element',[1] but it has been necessary to introduce some qualifications into this statement in inquiring how far it is true.

It is not true, in the first place, that *no* subjective activity is admitted by Plato. On the contrary, the virtue of Sophia, which is characteristic of the Platonic Polis, necessarily presupposes an activity of the subjective element. What is true is that this virtue, and the subjective freedom which it involves, is confined to the ruling class within the state, and that there is no corresponding freedom allowed to those who are members of the state only as subjects of it. There is subjective freedom in the imposition of form, but not in the submission to it. If, on the other hand, we determine 'the subjective element' to mean, not either of the first two parts of the soul, but the third or appetitive part, then it is true that this element is excluded from Plato's Polis, and that there is no such freedom either in ruler or in subject.

It is impossible to insist too strongly upon the difference

---

[1] Hegel adds that this defect, reflected in the Platonic theory, was characteristic also of the historical states of antiquity, and he thinks that the collapse of the ancient world was due to the irresistible outburst of the 'subjective principle' (which, he says, became the great principle of the Christian religion) when it could be suppressed no longer (*Philosophie des Rechts, Einleitung*, p. 13, §§ 185, 206). He is fond of contrasting with this defect of the Polis the tremendous strength of the modern State, which, by allowing a scope within itself for the exercise of subjective freedom, not only renders itself immune from the irruption of this principle, but draws vitality to itself from its activity.

We may perhaps point Hegel's contrast further by comparing the operation of Stasis in the ancient Polis with the operation of Party in the modern State. Stasis is the typical irruption of the 'subjective element' (it is for Plato the simple opposite of Dikaiosune; cf. iv. 444*b*, v. 464*d* ff.), and where it prevailed in a Polis, law ceased. But Party is not incompatible with the maintenance of law in a modern State; indeed Party Politics is the very process by which law is brought into being.

THE 'SUBJECTIVE ELEMENT'

between the two subjective activities, between that which Plato confines to the rulers and that which he excludes from the Polis. The former is the realization of the form, or universal, the latter is the direction of the soul upon a particular. Indeed, they are not only different, but incompatible, and the possibility of achieving the former depends upon the renunciation of the latter. A man can be taught to see the universal only by turning his back upon the illusions of sense perception, and he can be taught to will it only by abjuring the satisfactions of sensuous desire. That is why the rulers have to renounce the private affections of family life, the possession of private property, and, above all, participation in money-making or Chrematistike. The whole education of the guardians is a training in this renunciation; its end is the exercise of one 'subjective freedom', but its means is the surrender of the other.

From first to last Hegel confuses this distinction. He never sees that in charging Plato with excluding 'the subjective', he is bringing not one criticism, but two different criticisms against the Platonic theory. He is criticizing it in the first place on the ground that the subject has no share in the freedom which the ruler achieves in Sophia; and in the second place on the ground that there is no scope in the Polis for the exercise of the freedom which the ruler himself must renounce. Consequently in claiming for the State of his own theory that it avoids the defects of the Polis by being based upon 'subjective freedom', Hegel is claiming for the subject of the State two different and seemingly almost incompatible freedoms: (i) the freedom which consists in so willing the universal that the action is determined not simply by law, but by the concept of law, (ii) the freedom which consists in willing the particular, and of which it is the condition that the action shall be beyond the determination of any concept of law. But he never recognizes that these freedoms are not the same freedom, nor that the arguments for the introduction of the one are not adequate to justify the introduction of the other.

(i) The law is not imposed upon the subject of the State, as the Nomos is imposed upon the artisans of Plato's Polis by the activity of the ruler and without their active assent. The subject of the State must be free, and can be so only when he understands what he has to obey, and in so far as his understanding is the ground of his obedience. It makes a difference, says Hegel, 'whether I do a thing from habituation and custom or whether I do it from a whole-hearted conviction of its truth.'[1] It makes, in fact, all the difference between an act which is based upon the subjective activity of my own reason and one which is not, that is, between an act which is free and one which is not. The subject's right to freedom is thus the same as his 'right of insight'.[2] 'The right of the subjective will is that what it is to recognize as valid, shall approve itself to its insight as good.'[3] 'The principle of the modern world demands that whatever a man is to recognize must exhibit to him its title to recognition.'[4]

This is Hegel's enunciation of the grand principle of the 'Enlightenment', by which the individual judgement was set free from dependence upon the authority whether of a priest or of a prince. If we wish to express with precision what that principle involves and to escape from the windy eloquence in which talk of freedom is habitually clothed, we may do it by reference to the concepts whose meaning has been determined by the doctrine of the *Republic*.[5] The citizen of a State is free when his obedience to the law depends upon an activity of the reasoning element in him

---

[1] 'Von der Wahrheit desselben durchdrungen', § 140 z.
[2] 'Das Recht der Einsicht', § 132 A. [3] § 132; cf. § 228.
[4] 'Sich ihm als ein Berechtigtes zeige', § 317 z; cf. § 140 A.
[5] I own that I do not see how without this reference, or at least without a reference similarly historical, it can be done at all.

THE 'SUBJECTIVE ELEMENT' 83

identical with that which Plato perceived to be necessary in the ruler who administered it. This is a freedom in obeying, not a freedom to disobey (though it necessarily involves the possibility of disobedience). The Hegelian subject is determined in his actions by a universal order no less than the Platonic artisan, and he has to subdue his passions to this order no less than the Platonic auxiliary; only this order is one which can determine his actions only in so far as he knows it, and to which he can subdue his passions only in so far as he understands it. Thus every subject of the Hegelian State must possess the virtue of Sophia, which Plato could conceive as being exercised only at the moment in which its possessor ceased to be subject and became a ruler.

Since the subject in the State has to do what only the ruler need do in the Polis, namely to ascend to the conception of the universal and to will it in virtue of his knowledge, he has to undergo a training no less arduous than that which Plato thought was necessary to fit a man to be a ruler. The will for the universal can be attained only by a discipline in the renunciation of all particular desires. This discipline takes for Hegel the form of moral education, and when he speaks of morality[1] Hegel thinks always of Kant. The great task of morality, as Kant has conceived it, was that a man should free himself from all particular desires and elevate himself to the capacity of willing the universal of duty, and although Hegel is never tired of insisting that the sheerly universal moral law, as Kant had conceived it, is empty and therefore inadequate to serve as the standard of any action whatever, and that the only truly moral action is that which is devoted to the realization of the law of an actual state, he never wavers in the certainty that the subject must *first* have attained to the moral standpoint and that he can only then will that realization, because the law of an actual state is

[1] 'Moralität.'

itself universal, and the fulfilment of it something different from the satisfaction of any particular desire.

To try to give an adequate account of the relation of Kant's moral theory to Hegel's would be to stray beyond the limits of this work. But the reference to Kant may serve to enforce what I am here concerned to insist on, that the subjective element which is active in this freedom of the Hegelian subject is an element different from, even fundamentally opposed to, the subjective element which is the source of appetition; it is, as Kant says of 'respect', 'the conception of a worth *which thwarts my self-love*'.[1]

(ii) When he asserts that there is no scope for 'subjective freedom' in the Polis, Hegel no less often means something entirely different. He means that the Polis has no room for an activity of the appetitive element of the soul, which finds its natural satisfaction in Chrematistike. This freedom is quite different from that which we have hitherto considered; it is freedom of choice among alternatives left undetermined by reason and determined by nothing but desire. An act is free in the former sense when it is determined by the conception of a law; it is free in this latter sense when there is no law by the conception of which it can be determined. The condition of the former freedom is that the law should be reasonable, and understood by the subject to be reasonable; the condition of the latter is that the law should be so general in its terms that it leaves a sphere unpenetrated by its determination within which the individual can give rein to his arbitrary choice.

The great bulwark of this sphere of individual liberty against the encroachment of the law is the institution of private property, and the consequence of Plato's failure to appreciate its worth is his abolition of private property.

[1] *Foundation of the Metaphysic of Morals*, p. 21, note; Abbot's Tr., p. 18 (my italics).

THE 'SUBJECTIVE ELEMENT'

'The idea of the Platonic state involves, as a universal principle, this violation of the right of the person, namely that he is incapable of private property.'[1] Hegel does not distinguish in this respect between the status of rulers and of subjects in the Polis. If we make the distinction, we must say that the communism of property, which Hegel seems here to have in mind, cannot have extended beyond the guardian class; but that nevertheless, Hegel's criticism is true of the artisan class also, though upon a rather different ground.[2] The subject of the Polis can possess no such property as would constitute a bulwark of his freedom against governmental control; there is no sphere in which his action is not to be determined down to the minutest detail by the reasonable Nomos administered by the ruler. Nothing in the subject's life is free from the pitiless domination of reason, and one whole group of Hegel's criticisms are applicable to this lack of freedom in the subject. Thus he criticizes Plato for supposing that it is within the province of reason to determine such particular details of domestic life, as the manner in which babies are to be carried by their nurses;[3] and thus the great signs of lack of freedom in the Platonic Polis are that the individual subject is assigned to this or that trade or profession by the judgement of the rulers, not by his own choice,[4] and that the rulers prescribe to the subjects a particular service required from each as his contribution to a common undertaking instead of assessing (in taxation) the monetary value of the requisite contribution and leaving undetermined the choice of the work by which it is to be produced.[5]

In the State these choices are left undetermined by the

[1] § 46 A.
[2] The ruler is incapable of property on the ground on which the monk is incapable of it, the subject on the ground on which the slave is incapable of it.
[3] Vorrede, p. 14.   [4] § 206 A.   [5] § 299 A.

law, and it is the right of the individual to make them according to his wants. The freedom of the individual in the satisfaction of his desires and supply of his wants can be exercised only in a sphere of Chrematistike, or an economic sphere within the State, based upon property and dependent upon free labour, circumscribed and supported by the civil law, but owing its internal organization to no legal enactment, but to the unconscious operation of economic laws generated spontaneously in itself. The economic sphere must be released from the domination of political control in the free State, as desire must be released from the *dominium* of reason in the free man.

The two freedoms which Hegel confuses in his criticism of Plato under the common title of 'subjective freedom' I shall distinguish henceforth by the names of 'moral freedom' and 'freedom of desire' respectively. There are passages in Hegel's writings in which these two freedoms are not merely confused, but explicitly identified with one another. The passages are those devoted either explicitly or implicitly to a criticism of the moral theory of Kant,[1] in which the following argument recurs: Kant deems it essential to the purity of the moral will that it should be determined by a sheerly universal law, having a timeless being quite apart from the phenomenal realm and conceivable in entire distinction from any or all of the historical embodiments of law which come into being each at a particular time and place. Hegel denies that such a law is capable, owing to its abstractness, of determining a single action, and he exposes as a sham Kant's attempts to deduce particular duties from

[1] 'Wissenschaftliche Behandlungsarten des Naturrechts', in Lasson's *Hegels Schriften zur Politik und Rechtsphilosophie*, 2nd ed., pp. 349–54. Cf. *Phänomenologie*, vi. c. 'Der seiner selbst gewisse Geist; die Moralität.' Lasson's 2nd ed., pp. 388–434, and *Phil. d. Rechts*, §§ 139–40.

THE 'SUBJECTIVE ELEMENT' 87

the universal maxim of the law. A man may will to do right, and he will in fact perform some action, but the action which he does will not in fact be determined by the moral law which he has resolved to obey, because that law, being wholly indeterminate, cannot serve as a ground for doing one action rather than another. The unreflective man who has never consciously adopted this 'moral' standpoint is not exposed to this dilemma; his actions are determined by a law embodied in the statutes and the customs of the society to which he belongs, which, being thus in Hegel's language 'concrete', can and do determine the actions he performs. But the 'moral' man is beyond the standpoint at which he can accept the authority of any historical custom or positive law, and his freedom consists in setting in their place the universal law of duty. But since it appears that in throwing off allegiance to the concrete law he has emancipated himself from the only law which is capable of determining his action, and since, nevertheless, his action must be determined by something, it necessarily follows that his actions, even, or indeed especially, those done in pretence of obedience to the moral law, are determined in reality by those sheerly particular elements in his soul, desires, impulses, and passions, which escape direction by any law whatever. The will of good men who claim to have adopted the moral standpoint is saved from such excess only by the fact that it is still ruled unconsciously by traditional ethical principles to which they ought, if they were consistent, to attach no authority. Thus they interpret the law of duty in the light of ingrained ethical convictions, and delude themselves into the belief that they have deduced the latter from the law; as Kant imagines that he has derived the duty of respecting property from the maxim of the categorical imperative. The consistently moral man would not be thus deluded; his actions would therefore be determined solely by desire, and would differ from those of the profligate in nothing but in the hypocrisy of the pretence that they were determined by the law of duty. Thus Hegel concludes that the purely moral will is identical with the impulse of passion, and moral freedom indistinguishable from the 'empirical' freedom of following desire.

I suppose there is no reader of Hegel who has not felt in his heart that the argument for the identification of these opposites is a *tour de force*. It is not necessary for my purpose to examine it or to decide upon its validity; what I wish to point out is simply that the two things which in this argument are distinguished in order to be identified are in Hegel's criticisms of Plato not distinguished by him at all. When Hegel says that the State differs from the Polis in allowing its rights to the 'subjective element' or in being based upon 'subjective freedom', he must be held to mean by that term either one or other of the two things which we have found it to include, and it does make in this case a very considerable difference which is meant; whether, e.g., the State is held to differ from the Polis in allowing scope to the subject for the undetermined exercise of his desire, or in securing him an insight into the reason of the law which he is to obey. But which is meant is never decided by Hegel. He uses the phrases 'subjective freedom' and the like throughout the *Philosophy of Right* without exhibiting any consciousness that they are ambiguous, and while it can be determined on almost every occasion on which they occur in which sense the phrases are to be taken, the determination depends upon inference from the context.[1]

Both the impulse of appetite and the merely 'moral'[2] will fail, according to Hegel, to achieve either that genuine morality, which he calls Sittlichkeit, or the freedom which

---

[1] For evidence and illustration see Appendix E, p. 101 *inf.*
[2] 'Moralisch.'

THE 'SUBJECTIVE ELEMENT'

it is the essence of each to aim at, because neither issues in the realization of law. But neither is Sittlichkeit or freedom achieved by a realization of law which does not spring from these sources in the subjective will. What is 'sittlich' *is* subjective willing, only it is subjective willing of an objective law. The realization of Sittlichkeit thus demands something more than a certain condition of the subject's will. There must also be a law capable of governing his will and thus receiving its own fulfilment in his voluntary acts. No law which is merely ideal has this capacity, but only a law actually laid down and positively enforced. Therefore, if Sittlichkeit is to be possible, the laws of the actual state must be of such a nature that they are compatible both with freedom of conscience and with spontaneity of desire in the subject who obeys them. They must themselves possess an inherent reasonableness which the scrutiny of the enlightened judgement can reveal but not exhaust; and the order which they prescribe must be such that it does not suppress but satisfies the appetites which it regulates. It belongs to Hegel's metaphysics to deliver the guarantee that actual laws are of this nature, and we shall defer to the following chapter the consideration of this, the objective condition of the realization of Sittlichkeit; remarking here only that Hegel's failure to distinguish the two senses included in the term 'subjective will' infects his very notion of Sittlichkeit with ambiguity. The definition of Sittlichkeit as the realization by subjective will of a law which is right in itself[1] admits of two alternative interpretations, according as 'subjective will' is identified on the one hand with the moral, on the other with the appetitive will. In the former case Sittlichkeit will be realized when the moral agent recognizes in the law of the state an authority binding

---

[1] 'Das Sittliche ist subjektive Gesinnung, aber des an sich seienden Rechts', § 141 A.

upon his conscience; in the latter case, when the desires to satisfy wants are (not restrained, but) so harnessed that their very satisfaction is the vehicle of the realization of an order which the agent did not intend. Thus both conscience and appetite can become ethical will ('sittlicher Wille') when they are supplied with an appropriate framework of law; but they remain still alternative, not identical, means of its realization. When the moral agent is assured that the law of the state possesses all those claims upon his conscience which he has previously attributed only to the law of reason, then his obedience to the state satisfies his reason or his conscience, but not his desire. When the economic agent is left unfettered by the law in the supply of his wants, his desire is satisfied, but not his reason. Between these two wills, even when they are exercised within the state and have thus become ethical, there thus persists the difference, which we found to be of capital importance in another context,[1] that the former does, while the latter does not, will the law in virtue of a precedent knowledge of the end to be realized. If we regard the realization of the law as the end and the subjective satisfaction as the means to its fulfilment, then it is clear that only the moral man intends the end. Economic activity issues also, in fact, in the realization of law; but the intention of the economic agent is confined to the subjective satisfaction which is the means of its realization.

Because Hegel did not distinguish these two different meanings of 'ethical' will, it is not possible to give a definite answer to the question: Which is the properly Hegelian sense of the term? Primarily Hegel uses it in the former sense; 'sittlicher Wille' is the will of the moral man who has found in the state the law which he sought in vain in the supersensible region, and Sittlichkeit is the realization of

[1] Ch. I, p. 16.

THE 'SUBJECTIVE ELEMENT'

law by the will of a subject who intends the law which he realizes.[1] But he lapses frequently and without warning into the other usage of both these terms.[2]

We have considered so far only the contrast between the Hegelian State and the Platonic Polis in respect of this question of freedom. Freedom is satisfaction of the subjective element, and this satisfaction is achieved in Sittlichkeit. If we are to identify the subjective element with Plato's Third Part of the soul, it has appeared that the Polis admits no freedom of this element, and therefore achieves to this extent no Sittlichkeit. If we are to identify it with Plato's First Part of the soul, it has appeared that the realization of law demands no activity of this part in the soul of the subject, but only in the soul of the ruler, so that Sittlichkeit is excluded here also from the fulfilment of the law by the citizens, and is achieved only in the activity of the rulers in imposing law.

So far, then, it seems that the Polis is almost entirely lacking in what constitutes for Hegel the essence of the State. But when Hegel elucidates his conception of the State by contrast with Kant or the political theories of modern Empiricism, he refers to the Greek Polis, of which he takes Plato's *Republic* to be the ideal representation,[3] as that of all forms of society in which the nature of the State is most closely anticipated. It is not opposed to the State on the ground that it fails to realize Sittlichkeit; on the contrary it is ranked together with it as a form of Sittlichkeit, and distinguished from it only upon the ground that the Sittlichkeit which it achieved was 'immediate' ('unmittelbar') by contrast with the 'vermittelte' or 'absolute Sittlichkeit' of the State.

---

[1] Cf. especially §§ 142–57.
[2] See further Appendix E, p. 101 *inf*.
[3] Vorrede, p. 13, quoted, Appendix E, p. 101 *inf*.

Sittlichkeit is the product of a subjective activity,[1] and Hegel's use of this contrast therefore forbids the assumption that the criticisms which we have just considered completely represent his judgement upon Plato. If there was Sittlichkeit in the Polis, there must have been some activity of the subjective element, and therefore some freedom; so that it is necessary to consider how this judgement can be reconciled with the criticism that the Platonic Polis allowed no scope for 'subjective freedom'. The reconciliation becomes possible when we recall that the subjective elements denied satisfaction in the Polis were Plato's First and Third Parts of the soul; but the Second Part has a right to the title of a subjective element also, and its satisfaction also is a kind of freedom. Hegel's judgements upon Plato become consistent if he is understood to mean that the Polis realizes Sittlichkeit, and therefore freedom, in so far as it is based upon the virtue of the Second Part of the soul, but that it falls short of the State in providing no satisfaction for the First Part or for the Third. It will be necessary in order to make this clearer to devote some attention to what we have hitherto excluded from this chapter, namely to the position of the Second Class in the Polis, and to the virtue of the Second Part of the soul.

The Second Class of Plato's Polis occupies an ambiguous status. On the one hand, as a subdivision of the Guardian class, it is itself in relation to the Third Class a class of rulers. The education to which it is submitted is propaedeutic to the art of ruling, and the virtue of Andreia developed by this education is at once preparatory and auxiliary to the virtue of Sophia possessed by the genuine ruler: preparatory, because the information of the soul by virtuous habits is necessary if it is to be able to recognize the Idea of the Good when it is later disclosed to the enlightened reason,

[1] Cf. § 141 A, quoted p. 89, n. 1, *sup*.

THE 'SUBJECTIVE ELEMENT'

auxiliary because the philosopher returning from speculation to the practice of ruling will require the practical activity of the 'spirited part' to give effect in legislation to the ideas which he has apprehended theoretically.[1] So long as the Second Class is regarded exclusively in its relation to the Third, so long as the ethical education of Book iv[2] is held to be simply propaedeutic to the art of ruling and the virtue of Andreia simply auxiliary to that of Sophia, consideration of the Second Class in the city and of the Second Part of the soul necessitates no revision of the judgement which we have already formed upon the Polis. Since To Thumoeides is a subjective element, there will be freedom in the exercise of Andreia, which is its virtue—but the Auxiliaries will exercise this virtue and enjoy this freedom solely in so far as they are rulers. There will be no subjective activity in those upon whom their rule is imposed, and therefore nothing of what Hegel calls Sittlichkeit in the relation between them.

On the other hand, the Auxiliaries are themselves subjects in relation to the class above them, and when they are considered in this relation their peculiar virtue of Andreia acquires a value of its own not derivative simply from its being either preparatory or auxiliary to the exercise of Sophia. It becomes something which can be called in the strict sense of the term 'ethical virtue'.

The function of To Thumoeides in the achievement of this virtue[3] is to carry out the Logos or Form conceived by the lawgiver not in the political activity of embodying it in the institutions of a Polis, but in the properly ethical activity in which it is imposed upon the passions of the individual

---

[1] ... τὸ μὲν [sc. τὸ λογιστικόν] βουλευόμενον, τὸ δὲ [sc. τὸ θυμοειδές] προπολεμοῦν, ἑπόμενον τῷ ἄρχοντι καὶ τῇ ἀνδρείᾳ ἐπιτελοῦν τὰ βουλευθέντα. iv. 442b.   [2] Cf. especially 429 ff.
[3] For what follows see iv. 429a–430c, 439e–441d.

soul. The members of the Second Class do not realize Logos in the sense of apprehending it intellectually. They have not a rational insight into the right rule of life, but only 'right belief' which they must accept on trust from their rulers. But this right belief is not to be acquired by the mere submission of the soul, as passive subject-matter, to the operation of the ruler. It is not enough that the soul of the auxiliary should receive a form as the unresisting wax is stamped with an impression; there must be an active effort within the soul which is the subject of information to receive the form, to hold it fast,[1] and to maintain it against disintegrating influences within itself. The source of this effort is To Thumoeides, and the power of making it is called by Plato Andreia.[2]

That the virtue of Andreia in this sense, in which it approximates most nearly to the meaning of 'moral courage', has a value not derivative from its being propaedeutic to the acquisition of Sophia, will follow if it is admitted that the very possibility of its exercise depends upon the condition that the subject has only 'right belief', not clear and distinct apprehension, of the principles of conduct. If he not only believed that dishonour was a thing more to be feared than death, but understood how and why this was so, he could not show moral courage in resisting the solicitations of physical terror. Knowledge would dispel his temptations, and so put out of use the virtue of overcoming them.

However this may be, the point it is important to insist on here is that this virtue of Andreia implies a subjective

---

[1] διασώζεσθαι.

[2] See iv. 429–30, especially the striking phrase (429c) Σωτηρίαν ἔγωγε, εἶπον, λέγω τινὰ εἶναι τὴν ἀνδρείαν. In answer to the question Ποίαν δὴ σωτηρίαν; Socrates continues Τὴν τῆς δόξης τῆς ὑπὸ νόμου διὰ τῆς παιδείας γεγονυίας περὶ τῶν δεινῶν ἅ τέ ἐστι καὶ οἷα· διὰ παντὸς δὲ ἔλεγον αὐτῆς σωτηρίαν τὸ ἔν τε λύπαις ὄντα διασώζεσθαι αὐτὴν κα' ἐν ἡδοναῖς καὶ ἐν ἐπιθυμίαις καὶ ἐν φόβοις καὶ μὴ ἐκβάλλειν. Cf. 430b.

activity, exercised by the (political) subject in so far as he is subject, and that the presence of this virtue in the ruled institutes a relation between him and the ruler which is impossible in its absence. The ruler is related to the auxiliary not in the way in which he is related to the member of the Third Class, as craftsman to material, but as educator to pupil; the Andreia of the pupil, making him something more than mere subject-matter of information, is what makes this relation possible.

Sittlichkeit is realized in the relation of the First Class to the Second of Plato's Polis because this relation is based upon a subjective activity of the latter, who are therefore free in their submission. The contention that the subject of the Polis has no freedom can be maintained without qualification only so long as the members of the Third Class are held to be the only subjects; and it is inconsistent with the recognition that the Polis realizes a form of Sittlichkeit. When the Auxiliaries are regarded as subjects in the Polis, Hegel's criticism must be understood with a modification. These are not lacking in all subjective freedom, but they lack the freedoms which constitute the virtues of the First and the Third elements of the soul. The subject of the State will differ from the Platonic Auxiliary in that he adds to the ethical virtue of the latter *either* the freedom of insight into the rule which he obeys *or* the freedom of satisfying desire. The 'absolute' Sittlichkeit of the State will differ from the 'immediate' Sittlichkeit of the Polis in that, while in the latter the right rule is carried out in conduct, its execution is mediated in the former *either* by the insight of the subject into its rightness *or* by his free choice between alternatives. 'Either . . . or', because Hegel's thought is infected here with the old confusion. He does not distinguish these two kinds of subjectivity or these two modes of mediation.

We must beware, on the other hand, of the conclusion that it forms any part of Hegel's doctrine to substitute either or both of these new 'subjective freedoms' for the ethical virtue of the Platonic auxiliary, or even to suggest that it was the function of the State to realize the former to the exclusion of the latter. The latter without the former is only an 'immediate' form of Sittlichkeit; but the former without the latter are not forms of Sittlichkeit at all. Hegel's criticism of Plato for his omission of the former is introduced late into his ethical theory, and rather as a corrective of the opposite extreme; the theory was born of the criticism of the doctrines of his immediate predecessors, Rationalist and Empiricist respectively, for the opposite omission and for the false assumption that any freedom could be realized except upon the basis of an ingrained 'Ethos' or 'Sitte'.

This 'Ethos', the virtue of the Platonic Auxiliary, is the subjective, as the establishment of a reasonable law is the objective, condition of the realization of Sittlichkeit. In his insistence on the mutual dependence of these two conditions Hegel is reviving the truth of the Aristotelian principle that law is dependent upon Ethos to secure its enforcement.[1]

The freedom enjoyed by Plato's Auxiliaries we have distinguished by the title of the 'pagan' freedom, and this denomination may suggest the truth that this class of Plato's citizens represents the status of the citizen of an historical Greek polity. 'Freedom' was a condition of citizenship in a Greek Polis, and its exercise depended upon an ambiguity of status which, like that of Plato's Second Class, was not determined either as that of ruler or of ruled. For the maintenance of this freedom the citizens of the historical Polis were not self-sufficient, since it depended upon two condi-

---

[1] *Politics*, ii. 8 ὁ γὰρ νόμος ἰσχὺν οὐδεμίαν ἔχει πρὸς τὸ πείθεσθαι παρὰ τὸ ἔθος.

THE 'SUBJECTIVE ELEMENT'

tions which their own activity could not supply; first upon the satisfaction of their economic necessities by a servile class, secondly upon the pre-establishment of their constitution by a lawgiver. As the slave was below citizenship, so the lawgiver was above it; the slave was below humanity, and the lawgiver was half-divine. By these two dependences the free citizen of the Polis lacked the possibility of exercising the two freedoms characteristic of the member of the State; he lacked freedom in the satisfaction of his wants by being excluded from economic activity, and moral freedom by having withdrawn from his judgement the order determining his conduct.[1]

But it is a misjudgement of the *Republic* to make out, as Hegel does, that (not only Plato's Second Class, but) Plato's Polis as a whole is merely the retrospective representation of a form of society fast fading into history, only fortified anew against the intrusion of the principle which Plato perceived to have destroyed it.[2] This is to ignore what Plato himself claims[3] as the great achievement of the *Republic*, the distinction of the functions of rulers and of ruled, and it is to miss the significance of Plato's inclusion of the First and Third Classes within the ideal Polis. The essence of Plato's doctrine of Classes is that it goes beyond Greek practice in including as functions of organs within the state itself the

[1] Thus there was no sovereign legislative body in any Greek democracy. Above all, the dependence of the Greek upon oracles for the decision both of all important matters of state and of such private issues as fell beyond the scope of determination by Nomos, was the very abdication of moral freedom. Hegel continually emphasizes the significance of oracles in this connexion (cf., e.g., § 279 A and z). Socrates first had his oracle within him (the 'divine sign'), and thus anticipated the Christian freedom.

[2] Vorrede, p. 13, quoted Appendix E, p. 101 *inf.*, § 185 A, quoted ibid., p. 104. (If the destructive principle is the principle of individual self-determination discovered by Socrates, Plato is so far from rejecting it that he includes an entire class of Socrates' within his city.)

[3] *Timaeus* 17 C.

two activities, the divine and the servile, which the historical Greek Polis had failed to comprehend. The 'class state', first conceived in the Republic but realized much later,[1] represents thus a great advance towards freedom over the classless Polis of Greek history.

The further step, and that to which Hegel is pressing, is to demand that the functions of judgement and of economic satisfaction shall be exercised not merely by other classes within the same state, but by the same individual who as the auxiliary in Plato's Polis is subject of a naïvely ethical activity. It is the combination of this naïve submission to right with the satisfaction of reason or desire which first constitutes the 'absolute Sittlichkeit' and perfect freedom of the member of the State.

This further step involves the abolition of classes and the renaissance of the Greek ideal of a classless state.[2] But a renaissance is not a resurrection. The first and third classes are to be abolished not now through their exclusion from the state, but through the absorption of their functions by the second. The result of the absorption is that the State differs from the Polis not merely in the equal freedom of all individuals within its confines, but in the quality of the freedom which they exercise. It is not merely that the slave has been admitted to the franchise of the citizen; the liberty of the citizen has been enriched by including both the judgement of the philosopher and the economic activity of the slave.

---

[1] I suppose, if I may allow myself to guess, that its realization was the great achievement of the Middle Ages. The Greek Polis could not hold either the philosopher or the slave, but the Middle Ages included the Spirituality and the Commons as two estates within a larger community.

[2] As the historical movement which produced the modern State was both provoked by reaction against the Feudal System and inspired by the ideas of Greek democracy.

Appendix D
THE VIRTUE OF SOPHROSUNE IN PLATO

It may be suggested that the virtue of σωφροσύνη is an activity of the subjective element; that it is intended to represent an active acceptance of form by the subject, as distinct from the passive reception of which alone a material subject is capable. I am inclined to think that this suggestion is well founded; at least, if it is not, I am quite unable to distinguish σωφροσύνη from δικαιοσύνη itself. But if it is, then it might seem that a revision is demanded of the exposition of 'unmittelbare Sittlichkeit' which I have given in Ch. III; for σωφροσύνη will have a claim at least equal to that of ἀνδρεία to be regarded as the virtue of unreflective ethical conduct, and since σωφροσύνη is a virtue of all classes equally, it may appear that it was an error to confine the possibility of such conduct to the class which was constituted neither of rulers nor of subjects simply, but which occupied an ambiguous status between the two.

It must be replied that it was possible for Plato to represent σωφροσύνη as a universal virtue, common to all members of the Polis, only so long as he had not explicitly distinguished them into classes of rulers and ruled. The education by μουσική (iii. 389d–403c), which we have so far neglected to take any account of, is directed to the production of this virtue (Plato asserts this, 389d), and Plato's whole account of this education is marked by a failure to determine whether it is the education of a ruler or of a subject (thus in iii. 389d it is regarded as the 'chief part' of σωφροσύνη "ἀρχόντων ὑπηκόους εἶναι"; and cf. 390a. But it is implied quite clearly in other passages (394e, 395b, 396a, b) that this training in μουσική is an education of Guardians).

So soon as the differentiation of the city into separate classes of rulers who are not subjects and subjects who are not rulers became clear and explicit, both the virtue of σωφροσύνη and the discipline of μουσική by which it was produced, were bound to disappear. Σωφροσύνη can find no place in the souls of the rulers, because it is produced by the education of the sensuous element of the soul, whereas the function of ruling demands the subjection or even the eradication of this element, rather than its education. It can find no place in the souls of the ruled, because it must be assumed that the satisfaction of his appetitions in χρηματιστική is immediate and natural, neither requiring nor admitting an education, but at most availing itself of a technical training. Σωφροσύνη implies, in a word, that the sensuous element of the soul is educable, while the distinction of classes implies that it is not. The extent to which Plato was bound to modify his doctrine on this point, as the distinction between the classes became increasingly explicit, is well illustrated by the difference in the attitudes towards poetry (the chief instrument of a 'musical' education) expressed in Books iii and x respectively.[1] The distinction of classes in the state is intimately connected with that of parts in the soul, and it is significant that Plato in Book x explicitly attributes his new insight into the working of mimetic art to the intervening discovery of the three parts of the soul (595a; and cf. the whole argument beginning in 602c in which it is shown that μίμησις appeals to the irrational part of the soul).

The unreflective morality, therefore, which can be presented as the general virtue of all members of the city only so long as the explicit distinction into classes of rulers and ruled has not taken place, must be specialized after this distinction as the virtue of that single class which is neither simply regent nor simply subject; and there is to this extent an equal justification for holding the 'unmittelbare Sittlichkeit' of the Polis to be exemplified in either of the two virtues of ἀνδρεία or σωφροσύνη. The Hegelian doctrine of the 'absolute Sittlichkeit' of the State is even better illustrated if we take σωφροσύνη rather than ἀνδρεία as the example of the contrasted 'unmittelbare Sittlichkeit' of the Polis, because σωφροσύνη is not the virtue of a single

[1] Thus, e.g., in Book x poetry ὅση μιμητική is expelled entirely from the Polis (595a). The argument in Book iii (395b–398b) is that since the imitator becomes like what he imitates, the pupil must be confined to imitation of the good; i.e. μίμησις is recognized as an instrument of education, provided only that the models for imitation are properly selected.

THE 'SUBJECTIVE ELEMENT'

part of the soul, but a bond of unity of all the parts. Σωφροσύνη is possible for a man only so long as his position is not determined either as ruler or ruled. Once the distinction has been drawn (as it was the great achievement of the *Republic* itself to draw it), it is impossible to recapture this naïve virtue. It was the idea of the Hegelian 'Sittlichkeit' to redintegrate at the higher level of conscious achievement the primitive unity of the soul which was lost when σωφροσύνη was lost. The citizen of the State is not to recapture the ambiguous status of being *neither* ruler *nor* ruled (nor to alternate between the two situations by the fortunes of the lot), but he is to be himself at once *both* ruler *and* ruled. The difference between the naïve unity of the soul, which is possible before the separation of ruler and ruled has taken place, and the unity redintegrated when it has taken place, is the difference between the 'unmittelbare Sittlichkeit' of the citizen of the Polis and the 'vermittelte Sittlichkeit' of the citizen of the State.

APPENDIX E

HEGEL'S CRITICISMS OF PLATO, TOGETHER WITH OTHER REFERENCES TO 'SUBJECTIVE FREEDOM', ETC.; THEIR AMBIGUITY

Vorrede, pp. 13–14.

'Im Verlaufe der folgenden Abhandlung habe ich bemerkt, daß selbst die platonische Republik, welche als das Sprichwort eines leeren Ideals gilt, wesentlich nichts aufgefaßt hat als die Natur der griechischen Sittlichkeit, und daß dann im Bewußtsein des in sie einbrechenden tieferen Prinzips, das an ihr unmittelbar nur als eine noch unbefriedigte Sehnsucht und damit nur als Verderben erscheinen konnte, Plato aus eben der Sehnsucht die Hilfe dagegen hat suchen müssen, aber sie, die aus der Höhe kommen mußte, zunächst nur in einer äußeren besonderen Form jener Sittlichkeit suchen konnte, durch welche er jenes Verderben zu gewältigen sich ausdachte, und wodurch er ihren tieferen Trieb, die freie unendliche Persönlichkeit, gerade am tiefsten verletzte. Dadurch aber hat er sich als der große Geist bewiesen, daß eben das Prinzip, um welches sich das Unterscheidende seiner Idee dreht, die Angel ist, um welche damals die bevorstehende Umwälzung der Welt sich gedreht hat.'

§ 46 A. 'Die Idee des platonischen Staats enthält das Unrecht gegen die Person, des Privateigentums unfähig zu sein als allgemeines Prinzip.'

[What is the 'right' of the person here stated to be unsatisfied? Not, apparently, the right of judgement ('das Recht der Einsicht'), since this the guardians at least possess, and have achieved actually by means of their surrender of material possessions. Presumably, then, the right to satisfy desire.]

§ 121. 'Daß dies Moment der Besonderheit des Handelnden in der Handlung enthalten und ausgeführt ist, macht die subjektive Freiheit in ihrer konkreteren Bestimmung aus, das Recht des Subjekts, in der Handlung seine Befriedigung zu finden.'

§ 124 A. 'Das Recht der Besonderheit des Subjekts, sich befriedigt zu finden, oder, was dasselbe ist, das Recht der subjektiven Freiheit macht den Wende- und Mittelpunkt in dem Unterschiede des Altertums und der modernen Zeit. Dies Recht in seiner Unendlichkeit ist im Christentum ausgesprochen und zum allgemeinen wirklichen Prinzip einer neuen Form der Welt gemacht worden. Zu dessen näheren Gestaltungen gehören die Liebe, das Romantische, der Zweck der ewigen Seligkeit des Individuums u.s.f.,—alsdann die Moralität und das Gewissen, ferner die anderen Formen . . .'

[The demand that 'die Besonderheit des Handelnden' or 'des Subjekts' shall be satisfied in action is clearly capable of two interpretations, according to the meaning attached to 'die Besonderheit'. 'Die Besonderheit' is simply what we have called the subjective element of the soul; it may thus include equally what Plato designated τὸ λογιστικόν and what Plato designated τὸ ἐπιθυμητικόν, and the demand that it shall be satisfied in action will mean one or other of two

THE 'SUBJECTIVE ELEMENT' 103

quite different things, according as it is determined in the former sense or in the latter. If in the former sense, the 'particularity of the subject' will be satisfied in any action which is done because it is approved by his reason; if in the latter sense, it will be satisfied in any action which is done because its doing is desired. The general statements of Hegel in the two paragraphs last quoted admit equally of either interpretation; the specification in § 124 of 'die Moralität und das Gewissen' as types of action in which the particularity of the subject is satisfied, imply that he is here taking 'die Besonderheit' in the former sense.]

§ 132. 'Das Recht des subjektiven Willens ist, daß das, was er als gültig anerkennen soll, von ihm als gut eingesehen werde.'

[This leaves no room for doubt that the 'particularity of the subject' is to be identified with τὸ λογιστικόν.]

§ 136 z. 'Der Mensch ist als Gewissen von den Zwecken der Besonderheit nicht mehr gefesselt, und dieses ist somit ein hoher Standpunkt, ein Standpunkt der modernen Welt, welche erst zu diesem Bewußtsein, zu diesem Untergange in sich, gekommen ist.'

[Conscience is the σοφία of the moral subject; the 'subjective element' which receives satisfaction is still identified exclusively with τὸ λογιστικόν. Compare in a similar sense § 317 z: 'Das Prinzip der modernen Welt fordert, daß, was jeder anerkennen soll, sich ihm als ein Berechtigtes zeige.']

§ 140 A. 'Das subjektive Recht des Selbstbewußtseins, daß es die Handlung unter der Bestimmung, wie sie an und für sich gut oder böse ist, wisse . . .'

[Once more the right of the subject is the right that his reason shall be satisfied.]

§ 182. 'Die konkrete Person, welche sich als besondere Zweck ist, als ein Ganzes von Bedürfnissen und eine Vermischung von Naturnotwendigkeit und Willkür, ist das eine Prinzip der bürgerlichen Gesellschaft—aber die besondere Person als wesentlich in Beziehung auf andere solche Besonderheit, . . .'

§ 182 z. 'Die Schöpfung der bürgerlichen Gesellschaft

gehört übrigens der modernen Welt an, welche allen Bestimmungen der Idee erst ihr Recht widerfahren läßt.'

§ 185 A. 'Die selbständige Entwickelung der Besonderheit (vergl. § 124 Anm.) ist das Moment, welches sich in den alten Staaten als das hereinbrechende Sittenverderben und der letzte Grund des Untergangs derselben zeigt. . . . Plato in seinem Staate stellt die substantielle Sittlichkeit in ihrer idealen Schönheit und Wahrheit dar, er vermag aber mit dem Prinzip der selbständigen Besonderheit, das in seiner Zeit in die griechische Sittlichkeit hereingebrochen war, nicht anders fertig zu werden, als daß er ihm seinen nur substantiellen Staat entgegenstellte, und dasselbe bis in seine Anfänge hinein, die es im Privateigentum (§ 46 Anm.) und in der Familie hat, und dann in seinen weiteren Ausbildung als die eigene Willkür und Wahl des Standes u.s.f., ganz ausschloß. Dieser Mangel ist es, der auch die große substantielle Wahrheit seines Staates verkennen und denselben gewöhnlich für eine Träumerei des abstrakten Gedankens, für das, was man oft gar ein Ideal zu nennen pflegt, ansehen macht. Das Prinzip der selbständigen in sich unendlichen Persönlichkeit des Einzelnen, der subjektiven Freiheit, das innerlich in der christlichen Religion und äußerlich, daher mit der abstrakten Allgemeinheit verknüpft, in der römischen Welt aufgegangen ist, kommt in jener nur substantiellen Form des wirklichen Geistes nicht zu seinem Rechte.'

§ 185 z. 'Wenn der platonische Staat die Besonderheit ausschließen wollte, so ist damit nicht zu helfen, denn solche Hilfe würde dem unendlichen Rechte der Idee widersprechen, die Besonderheit frei zu lassen. In der christlichen Religion ist vornehmlich das Recht der Subjektivität aufgegangen, wie die Unendlichkeit des Für-Sich-Seins, und hierbei muß die Ganzheit zugleich die Stärke erhalten, die Besonderheit in Harmonie mit der sittlichen Einheit zu setzen.'

§ 206. 'Der Stand, als die sich objektiv gewordene Besonderheit, teilt sich so einerseits nach dem Begriffe in seine allgemeinen Unterschiede. Andererseits aber, welchem besonderem Stande das Individuum angehöre, darauf haben Naturell, Geburt und Umstände ihren Einfluß, aber die letzte und

THE 'SUBJECTIVE ELEMENT' 105

wesentliche Bestimmung liegt in der subjektiven Meinung und der besonderen Willkür, die sich in dieser Sphäre ihr Recht, Verdienst und ihre Ehre gibt, so daß, was in ihr durch innere Notwendigkeit geschieht, zugleich durch die Willkür vermittelt ist und für das subjektive Bewußtsein die Gestalt hat, das Werk seines Willens zu sein.'

A. 'Auch in dieser Rücksicht tut sich in bezug auf das Prinzip der Besonderheit und der subjektiven Willkür der Unterschied in dem politischen Leben des Morgenlandes und Abendlandes, und der antiken und der modernen Welt hervor. Die Einteilung des Ganzen in Stände erzeugt sich bei jenen zwar objektiv von selbst, weil sie an sich vernünftig ist; aber das Prinzip der subjektiven Besonderheit erhält dabei nicht zugleich sein Recht, indem z. B. die Zuteilung der Individuen zu den Ständen den Regenten, wie in dem platonischen Staate (de Rep. III, p. 320, ed. Bip. T. vi.), oder der bloßen Geburt, wie in den indischen Kasten, überlassen ist. So in die Organisation des Ganzen nicht aufgenommen und in ihm nicht versöhnt, zeigt sich deswegen die subjektive Besonderheit, weil sie als wesentliches Moment gleichfalls hervortritt, als Feindseliges, als Verderben der gesellschaftlichen Ordnung (s. § 185 Anm.), entweder als sie über den Haufen werfend, wie in den griechischen Staaten und in der römischen Republik, oder wenn diese als Gewalt habend oder etwa als religiöse Autorität sich erhält, als innere Verdorbenheit und vollkommene Degradation, wie gewissermaßen bei den Lakedämoniern und jetzt am vollständigsten bei den Indern der Fall ist.—Von der objektiven Ordnung aber in Angemessenheit mit ihr und zugleich in ihrem Recht erhalten, wird die subjektive Besonderheit zum Prinzip aller Belebung der bürgerlichen Gesellschaft, der Entwickelung der denkenden Tätigkeit, des Verdienstes und der Ehre. Die Anerkennung und das Recht, daß, was in der bürgerlichen Gesellschaft und im Staate durch die Vernunft notwendig ist, zugleich durch die Willkür vermittelt geschehe, ist die nähere Bestimmung dessen, was vornehmlich in der allgemeinen Vorstellung Freiheit heißt (§ 121).'

And cf. in a closely similar sense § 262, and § 262 z.

§ 299 A. 'Plato läßt in seinem Staate die Individuen den besonderen Ständen durch die Oberen zuteilen und ihnen ihre besonderen Leistungen auflegen (vergl. § 185 Anm.); in der Feudalmonarchie hatten Vasallen ebenso umbestimmte Dienste, aber auch in ihrer Besonderheit, z. B. das Richteramt u.s.f. zu leisten. . . . In diesen Verhältnissen mangelt das Prinzip der subjektiven Freiheit, daß das substantielle Tun des Individuums, das in solchen Leistungen ohnehin seinem Inhalte nach ein Besonderes ist, durch seinen besonderen Willen vermittelt sei;—ein Recht, das allein durch die Forderung der Leistungen in der Form des allgemeinen Wertes möglich, und das der Grund ist, der diese Verwandlung herbeigeführt hat.'

[If the group of passages quoted earlier in this appendix (§§ 121, 124 A, 132, 136 Z, 140 A) be contrasted with those last quoted (§§ 182, 182 Z, 185 A and Z, 206, 206 A, 299 A),[1] two things become evident:

(i) Hegel is not conscious that he is formulating in the passages of the latter group a doctrine in any way different from that already presented in those of the former group. (Thus in the course of § 206 he refers for confirmation to §§ 121 and 120 A.) The doctrine common to both groups is that the law of the State (the universal) must be realized by an activity originating in the subject (the particular) upon which it is imposed. We may relate this doctrine to the terms of our previous discussions by pointing out two implications; it is implied that this realization of law in a State differs (a) from that realization of a universal which constitutes (on the Aristotelian doctrine) the genesis of a natural object, (b) from that realization of form which is the production of an object of art. In the former the spring of activity lies wholly in the form, in the latter it lies in the artist in so far as he is dominated by the conception of the form; but in neither case does it lie in the subject-matter upon which the form is imposed.

[1] § 46 A, quoted earlier, belongs also to this group. Vorrede, p. 13, is not sufficiently determinate to be assigned to either.

THE 'SUBJECTIVE ELEMENT'

This activity of the subject, then, in the realization of law is what Hegel calls 'subjektive Freiheit', and is what he recognizes as the distinguishing characteristic of the modern State. The other phrases which he uses (throughout the passages of both groups) are well adapted to express the same meaning. Thus this subjective activity may properly be called 'dies Moment der *Besonderheit* des Handelnden in der Handlung' (§ 121; cf. § 185 A, Z, 206) since the 'subjective element' is the particular element (see Ch. III, p. 73 *sup.*); and it has an intelligible sense to say that such activity constitutes a 'satisfaction of the individual', and that its infringement is a denial of the 'right of the individual'. But—

(ii) All these terms—'the subjective element', 'the individual', 'the particularity of the subject'—are ambiguous. If we revert for a moment to the terms of the Platonic psychology, it is plain that 'the subjective element' may designate the *whole* of that element in the soul which is distinguishable from its form, i.e. it may mean *all* or *any* of the three 'parts of the soul', τὸ λογιστικόν, τὸ θυμοειδές, τὸ ἐπιθυμητικόν, in contrast with the form of their tripartite organization. If we leave τὸ θυμοειδές out of account, it is plain that τὸ λογιστικόν and τὸ ἐπιθυμητικόν have their modern (at least their Hegelian) counterparts in conscience and desire respectively. 'The subjective element' is a term which may properly be used to designate either of these. Whether the action in which I realize the law is done because I judge it to be demanded by my duty, or because I am impelled to do it in pursuit of my interest, in either case the spring of the action has been in me, the subject, and in either case my right as an individual to 'subjective freedom' has been satisfied in the activity. It is nevertheless of the utmost importance to distinguish in any given action which of these two 'subjective elements' has been satisfied. It may be that an action dictated by conscience and an action instigated by desire are alike acts of free will; but it remains true that they are not identical, but are alternative realizations of freedom, and are, at least prima facie, mutually exclusive alternatives.

This is the distinction which Hegel does not draw. He uses the indeterminate phrases, 'subjective Besonderheit' and the rest, as though they were fully determinate. In every passage in which he proceeds beyond a very general phraseology it is necessary to assign to these terms one of the two possible alternative meanings, but it is by no means always the same meaning, and only the context can determine which in any given instance is to be supplied.

Thus in the former of the two groups of passages which I have distinguished above, 'the subjective' means conscience, or the moral will, or the will directed upon the universal. 'Sittlichkeit' is the realization of positive law in an act of will. If we distinguish as the two elements of this total reality the law which is willed and the will which wills it, the 'subjective element' is the latter. Of the two elements into which the self is divided in the Kantian morality, the moral will and the natural passions, the 'subjective element' in these passages of Hegel is identified exclusively with the former.

But in the latter group of passages the 'subjective element' does not mean the will for the universal at all; it means the natural will, or the will directed upon the particular. The 'Person', in whom this will is embodied, is stated to be a 'totality of wants and a mixture of natural necessity and caprice' (§ 182). His freedom is secured only in an action which originates in his 'besondere Willkür' (§ 206); and we are actually given as a definition of freedom 'daß, was in der bürgerlichen Gesellschaft und im Staate durch die Vernunft notwendig ist, zugleich durch *die Willkür* vermittelt geschehe' (§ 206 A). But 'Willkür', the will for the sheerly particular, and the moral will, which was connoted by the 'subjective element' in the former group of passages, are so different that they are mutually exclusive. The latter may be called 'besonderer Wille' (see § 288 A), in the sense that it is the will of a particular subject; but the latter alone is 'besonderer Wille' also in the further sense that it is will for a particular object.

The passages in which these terms are used do not fall in

the arrangement of the *Philosophie des Rechts* quite so clearly into two groups as my selection would seem to imply; although it is natural that the former meaning should predominate in passages within the section 'Die Moralität' (§§ 105–41), and the latter within the section 'Die Bürgerliche Gesellschaft' (§§ 182–256). For passages in which the two meanings appear confused within the limits of a single context, cf. §§ 148–9; and perhaps §§ 260 and z, 261 and z.]

IV

LAW AS THE CONDITION OF FREEDOM IN THE STATE

BOTH the 'moral' will and the impulse of appetite become 'sittlich' by being united with that settled ethical disposition which constituted civic virtue in an ancient state; this ethical disposition in its turn is perfected by the addition of 'subjective freedom' in being united with either one of these.

Hegel designates the product of either combination indifferently by the single term 'sittlicher Wille'; but we shall require two terms in order to distinguish what he confuses, and I shall henceforth use the two names 'ethical' and 'economic' will to designate respectively the combination of (naïve) ethical disposition with (1) moral insight, and (2) desire. I shall distinguish similarly as 'ethical' and 'economic' freedom respectively the fulfilment achieved on the one hand by morality, on the other by desire in the Sittlichkeit of the State.[1]

We have now to consider the conditions which make

---

[1] It is the best justification of a terminology that it proves convenient and avoids ambiguity, but it may nevertheless appear at first sight an unhappy choice to have used to designate one of the two classes of the acts which Hegel embraces under the term 'Sittlichkeit', a translation of the term ('ethical' = 'sittlich') which Hegel uses to include them both. In fact, however, what Hegel *means* by 'sittlich' is almost always what I have defined as 'ethical'. His confusion is less often a confusion in the connotation of the term than an illicit extension of its denotation to include a class of acts (the 'economic') which do not conform to its definition.

'Ethical' will, in the sense in which I shall use it henceforth, must of course be distinguished from the naïvely ethical will characteristic of the citizen of the ancient Polis; but the context will suffice to preclude ambiguity here.

The relation of the distinction now introduced to that made in the

FREEDOM IN THE STATE

either combination possible; in other words, the conditions which enable the subject of the State to be free, as the subject of the Polis was not, whether in the sense of ethical or in that of economic freedom.

As the virtue of the subject of the Polis depended upon Nomos, so that of the subject of the State depends upon Law, and in order to discover the conditions of the freedom which is peculiar to the latter, we must inquire into the characteristics which distinguish the law of the State from the Nomos of the Polis.

In the two thousand years which intervened between Plato and Hegel a revolution had taken place not only in political philosophy but in every other province of thought. In order to understand this revolution, it would be necessary first to have understood at least the whole history of philosophy between Plato and Hegel, a task quite ludicrously beyond the plan of a work like this, which is based upon the pretence that the intervening period can be ignored; but it may be possible briefly to designate some of its results.

I think the essence of it can best be expressed by saying that the conception of Form as the principle of reason and order in the universe was replaced by the conception of Law. To both of these, to form as well as to law, we apply the same term 'the universal', and we thereby obscure to ourselves the great difference between them. For instance (to illustrate the distinction from the sphere of natural science) any particular material object we conceive as subject to the

previous chapter (p. 86 *sup.*) between the moral will and appetite, and between 'moral freedom' and 'freedom of desire', is simply that the ethical and the economic will *are* the moral will and appetite respectively in so far as these are satisfied within the conditions of Sittlichkeit; and that the ethical and economic freedoms are nothing but the fulfilment within the State of the moral and appetitive 'freedoms' which are necessarily illusory without it.

operation of innumerable laws. Its position and weight are determined by the law of gravitation, its movement by laws of mechanics, its temperature by laws of radiation, the appearance of its surface by laws of optics. All these laws are, in relation to the particular object, universal, in the sense that their operation is not private or peculiar to it, but extends equally to all other objects in so far as they are material. That is the universal as law, and we conceive Nature as a realm of law when we conceive it as an interrelated system of such laws.

But we may conceive the universal of any particular object quite otherwise; we may conceive it as the *kind* to which the particular belongs. In this sense 'desk' will be the universal of 'this desk', 'stone' the universal of 'that stone', 'dog' the universal of Fido. The meaning of every concrete common noun is universal in this sense, because it is applicable always not merely to one particular but to all particulars of a kind. The particulars are said to be subsumed under the universal which designates their kind; and this universal is then found to be itself capable of further subsumption under a superordinate universal, as species under a genus, this genus again under a higher genus, and so on upwards until a *summum genus* is reached. This is the conception of the universal as form, and of Nature not as a realm of law but as a realm of form, hierarchical or architectonic, in which the most general idea determines itself through successive differentiations to the variety of its *infimae species*. According to the former conception the individual is a meeting-place of laws, according to the latter an embodiment of form.

The revolution which I have mentioned took place when the former of these conceptions superseded the latter, and men began to look for principles of reason in Nature in general laws instead of in generic forms. When this

FREEDOM IN THE STATE

happened at the close of the Middle Ages the modern physical science of nature came into being.

An analogous revolution took place in other spheres of thought besides that of natural science. In Ethics the conception of the supreme form or 'architectonic end' as the principle of conduct gave way to the conception of the moral law, and in political philosophy the conception of Nomos, or reasonable form,[1] as the principle of order in human society was replaced by the conception of Law, or of what Hegel calls 'Gesetz'.[2]

The conditions of realizing *both* of the 'subjective freedoms' in the subject lie in those characters by which law as 'Gesetz' is differentiated from 'Nomos'. These characters are, first, its objectivity to the reason of the subject; secondly, the generality of its application. They are the characters which distinguish Law, as Nomos was never distinguished, from custom; for custom may operate in a subject without having been made the object of his conscious apprehension, and it may determine not merely the general nature but the particular detail of his act.

In order to throw these two characteristics of law into the strongest possible relief, I will endeavour first to illustrate them in a conception of law which is not Hegelian, but which, because it stands at a still further remove from Plato, exhibits them with a clarity and a crudity not found in Hegel himself; I mean the (Empiricist) conception of law as being in its essence a command.[3]

This doctrine implies that it belongs to the very essence

---

[1] νόμος τε καὶ λόγος. *Rep.* ix. 587c.

[2] I do not mean, I need hardly add, that Law has the same meaning in the three spheres of Natural Science, Ethics, and Political Philosophy; but only that it is in all three equally to be contrasted with Form.

[3] 'Law properly is the word of him that by right hath command over others.' Hobbes, *Leviathan*, I. xv.

of law to be *positive*; that is to say, that it owes its character as law precisely to that element within it which is not penetrable by the speculative reason.[1] It is thus in direct opposition to the conception of law as Nomos, since the essence of Nomos is the reasonable principle (Logos) which it embodies. To this alone it owes its authority, and this principle is wholly transparent to the speculative intelligence. Opaque to reason are only the accidents of its historical realization, and these are an inevitable imperfection, not the ground of its authority.[2] But to Hobbes (to take him once more as the representative of the opposite view) a principle lacks authority to determine conduct so soon as it is seen to be no more than a principle of pure reason. Thus the 'dictates of Reason' which 'men use to call by the name of lawes' (the so-called laws of nature) are improperly so called, precisely because they are logically deducible from principles of reason; 'they are but conclusions, *or Theoremes* concerning what conduceth to the conservation and defence of themselves'.[3] Hobbes adds that, 'if we consider the same Theoremes as delivered by the word of God, that by right commandeth all things; then they are properly called Lawes'. They are constituted laws, that is to say, not by being reasonable, but by being commanded; and what makes them obligatory upon the will of the subject commanded is their source in the will (not in the reason) of the commander.

A command exhibits both the characters of objectivity to the subject and of generality or abstractness by which Law is distinguished from Nomos.

(i) Objective means object to the theoretical understanding, and it is the peculiarity of a command that an under-

---

[1] I define the term 'positive' in this sense.
[2] Because of this opacity, the subject can have only ὀρθὴ δόξα.
[3] Hobbes, *Leviathan*, I. xv (my italics).

FREEDOM IN THE STATE

standing of it by the person commanded is a condition essential to its being carried out at all. This is by no means true of custom, for an action may be determined by custom without the agent's awareness of the custom by which it is determined; and though he may hereafter acquire this insight, still, since the action might equally be performed without it, it remains true that the insight is epiphenomenal, and not a condition *sine qua non* of the carrying out of the custom in action. Whereas it is obvious that a command can determine any action whatever only in so far as it is understood by the person commanded, no less than by the person commanding. So that it is involved in the very nature of a command that it presupposes in him who is subject to it at least an activity of understanding.

(ii) It is a further characteristic of a command that it is always general or abstract; that is to say, that it can never comprehend the whole detail of the act in which it is to be fulfilled. A Nomos imparted by habituation[1] and producing an informed disposition[2] in the subject submitted to it can determine the particular detail of the acts arising from it. Not merely what is done, but the style and manner of doing it will be referable to the tradition which gives it birth; as the work of an artist betrays his school no less in the characteristic details of his execution than in the general conception of his design. But in an act determined by a command there must always be a sharp line of distinction between the essence of what is commanded and the indifferent details of its execution. The latter can never be determined by the command, however specific the command may be. I am commanded, e.g., to dig a particular garden, or even a particular plot within it. But neither the command nor my willingness to obey it can determine precisely the gesture with which I wield the spade, nor the exact spot of earth in

[1] ἐθισμός. [2] ἕξις.

which I place it. If we could suppose my actions determined apart from my initiative down to the limit of particular detail, then I should have ceased to be even a slave, and should have become a tool or a machine; i.e. the relation of command, that between master and servant or commander and commanded, would have disappeared and would have been replaced by that of operator and instrument.[1]

The fulfilment of a command, therefore, requires in the subject of it the exercise of an initiative in determining those particular details of the performance which the command itself cannot determine without ceasing to be a command. It is clear that this initiative is quite different from the resolution of the subject's will to obey the command, which I have mentioned above, since that resolution can determine nothing not determined by the command. That is a will to submit to determination by the command, this to supply what the command leaves undetermined. As that is analogous to Hegel's ethical will, so this is analogous to his economic will, and I have tried to show that its exercise is correlative to the character of generality or abstractness in law.

Since Hegel himself proclaims it as the differentia of his political philosophy that it is founded upon the 'subjective freedom' of the individual, and since the objectivity and the generality, which have been found to be correlative to this freedom of the subject in one or other of its alternative senses, are consequent upon the character, exhibited by a command, of being positive, it will be profitable to inquire

[1] The Greeks never realized this difference between a slave and a tool. 'ὁ γὰρ δοῦλος ἔμψυχον ὄργανον, τὸ δ' ὄργανον ἄψυχος δοῦλος.' Aristotle, *Eth. Nic.* viii. 11. The whole of that development of political philosophy to which this chapter is devoted is based ultimately on the recognition, which the Greeks lacked, that freedom is compatible with obedience to command.

FREEDOM IN THE STATE

whether and in what sense Hegel recognizes the positivity of law. Will he be found to go beyond Plato in his doctrine of law, as he goes beyond him in his doctrine of freedom?

Hegel will not go with Hobbes to the length of asserting that it belongs to the essence of law to be positive. His thought is far too deeply rooted in the Rationalist tradition to permit the conclusion that there is something impenetrable by the speculative intelligence not merely in the particular circumstances of the application of law, not merely in the temporal accidents of its historical embodiment, but in its very being as law.[1] The very possibility of a 'Philosophy of Right' presupposes that the system of law and constitution of the State is in its main outlines deducible by a necessity of reason from the nature of Being as such. The 'Philosophy of Right' finds its place in the Hegelian system within the Philosophy of Spirit, which is in its turn only the third and final stage of that development through which speculative reason, starting in Logic from the concept than which there can be none simpler, is driven by the necessity of its own dialectic; and Hegel never doubts that the same capacity of metaphysical deduction which makes law intelligible to the reason of the philosopher, makes it also obligatory upon the will of the moral subject.[2]

The doctrine so far is wholly Platonic. For Plato also the nature of the Polis, in so far as it was just, must be derivable from the nature of being, and the process of this derivation had been called by him also Dialectic.

This philosophical deduction of law can extend, according to Hegel, no further than to the specification of its

[1] Hegel's repudiation of this suggestion is famous. See Einleitung, p. 14: 'Darauf kommt es dann an, in dem Scheine des Zeitlichen und Vorübergehenden die Substanz, die immanent, und das Ewige, das gegenwärtig ist, zu erkennen' and ff.

[2] See especially §§ 142–8; and p. 124, n. 1, *inf.*

general outlines.[1] The further particularization which is necessary for its concrete embodiment as the law of this or that individual state is the object not of a philosophical, but only of an historical understanding;[2] and Hegel emphatically repudiates the notion that an historical study of the genesis of an actual system of law can take the place of this metaphysical deduction,[3] or that the historical necessity which alone such a study could reveal, could serve, as the metaphysical necessity disclosed by philosophical speculation serves, as the ground of its moral authority.[4]

Positivity, therefore, in the sense in which that is positive which is opaque to speculative reason, is denied by Hegel to belong to the essence of law, and is confined to the accidents of its historical actualization. But even such positive enactments have, if not a reasonable, at least an historical necessity, and are objects of a study which, if not philosophical, is at least a science. An element opaque to *all* understanding, what Hegel calls the 'purely positive element of law', enters only at a further stage, namely in administration, or the application of law to the individual case.[5] In application the universal of law must become particularized and must step thereby 'into the realm of the accidental, which cannot be determined by the concept'.[6] For the particular detail of application, therefore, the subject can

---

[1] It can proceed, we must assume, precisely down to that degree of detail to which it is developed by Hegel in the Philosophy of Right; cf. § 3 A, p. 21.

[2] § 3. It is the object of 'die positive Rechtswissenschaft' (ibid., p. 20); study of it is a 'rein geschichtliche Bemühung' (p. 20).

[3] § 212 A, 258 A, p. 196.

[4] § 3, cf. § 148 A.

[5] 'In dieser Zuspitzung des Allgemeinen, nicht nur zum Besonderen sondern zur Vereinzelung, d.i. zur unmittelbaren Anwendung, ist es vornehmlich, wo das *rein Positive* der Gesetze liegt.' § 214 A.

[6] 'Damit tritt es in die Sphäre des durch den Begriff Unbestimmten'. § 214.

demand no reason, but must submit his will therein to the fiat of a will.[1]

Both in this delimitation of a sphere of particular detail, to which determination 'by the concept' cannot reach, and in this recognition that the particular, even lacking such determination, is still not wholly undetermined, but is intelligible as the product of historical causes, it is possible to discuss a significant difference between the Hegelian and the Platonic theory, but I wish, while showing this difference, still to concentrate attention upon their agreement. They agree in so far as Hegel denies that there is any element opaque to the speculative reason in the being of law as such and considered apart either from the accidents of its embodiment or from the detail of its administration.

But although Hegel denies that it belongs to the essence of law to be positive, he insists that it belongs to the essence of law to be 'posited'. 'Gesetz' is the German word for 'law' and 'setzen' for 'posit', and Hegel lays stress upon this etymological affinity as being significant of a real connexion.[2] How is this activity of 'positing' to be understood? And how is it possible to conceive law as the product of such an activity without ascribing to it that character as *positive* which must belong to it so soon as it is conceived as the product of an activity of will? 'Positing' is for Hegel an act rather of codifying, than of laying down, the law. It is the act by which the 'right',[3] which has been valid for a people in the form of customary law is formulated as a public system of intelligible rules presented to the understanding

---

[1] If an offender is to be punished, e.g., the precise amount of his punishment must be determined, but it is capable of being determined by no reasonable principle. If forty lashes are inflicted, no reasoning can show that forty-one would have been too many and thirty-nine too few for his offence. Here the judge must decide, and the offender submit, without reason. § 214 A. [2] § 211.
[3] 'Das Recht.'

of the subjects, so that their conformity may be based henceforth no longer upon unreflective custom, but on recognition of these rules as right.[1] In other words, 'positing' is understood by Hegel as an act not of will but of thought[2] (it is a task for the lawyer rather than for the lawgiver)—and therefore it imports into its product no element impenetrable by thought. There are thus two main respects in which Hegel's doctrine of law differs from Plato's.

(i) He regards law as the product of an activity of 'positing', which yet imports into its nature no element impenetrable by the speculative reason.

(ii) He so limits the competence of speculative reason in the determination of law, as to make it stop short of the particular detail of its actualization.

This is to ascribe to law precisely those two characters of (i) objectivity and (ii) generality which are the conditions of the freedom of the subject in one or other of the two senses of the word. Thus (i) the right of the subject to ethical freedom is satisfied by the condition that the law should be 'posited', i.e. *published*,[3] or set over against the subject as an objective *corpus juris*. Such a legal system must be assumed to be, no less than the Nomos of a just Polis, a necessary development of reasonable principles; but this objectifica-

---

[1] § 211; cf. § 215, 224.

[2] Cf. his words in § 211 A: 'Etwas als Allgemeines setzen ... ist bekanntlich Denken'. On the whole the character which Hegel attributes to law, that of being 'posited', is the character by which Roman Law differs from Greek. Both the achievement and the defect of Hegel's doctrine of law may be summed up by saying that he has absorbed the Roman conception of law, but has failed to absorb the Judaic. Cf. pp. 135 ff. *inf.*

[3] §§ 211, 215–17; cf. § 349 and § 132 A, p. 111. This publication will only be fully secured if the processes by which the law is enforced are public also (§§ 224, 228). It will appear later (cf. Ch. V, pp. 168 ff. *inf.*) that a like publicity must be extended on like grounds from the judicial to the properly political sphere, i.e. from the process of the enforcement of law to the process of its constitution and modification.

tion, which differentiates it from the Nomos, makes it incapable of determining immediately the action of a subject. It can be carried out by him in action only in so far as its reason is recognized by himself, and his will determined by the recognition. But such an act is an act of (ethical) freedom.

And (ii) the right of the subject to economic freedom is secured by the condition that the determination of law by reason shall stop short of the particular detail of its execution.

It will be convenient in what follows to consider separately the two characters of objectivity and generality of law, and with each separately the subjective freedom of which it is the condition.

I

Hegel is at one with Plato in maintaining that the law of the just state is determined, at least in its main outlines, by a process of logic, and he adopts the Platonic term, dialectic, to designate this process. But there is a difference between the Hegelian dialectic and the Platonic, and this difference in metaphysical doctrine will be found to be the ground of that difference in their political philosophies which we have mentioned: namely, that Hegel does and Plato does not assign ethical freedom to the subject of the state.

The difference lies in this, that for Plato the nature of being, or the idea which is the object of philosophical understanding, is in itself changeless and without process. The process[1] which constitutes dialectic falls wholly within the understanding of the philosopher. It is he who proceeds by the criticism and negation[2] of inadequate definitions of being[3] to the first principle which *is* absolutely[4] and is there-

---
[1] For what follows, see *Rep.* vi. 511.   [2] ἀναιρῶν (see vii. 533c).
[3] ὑποθέσεις.   [4] ὄντως ὄν.

fore knowable absolutely.[1] It is he, again, who proceeds in the reverse direction downwards to the reaffirmation of the positions previously discarded, not now as absolute but as qualified being and as intelligible with this qualification.[2] And it is he who must take, if it is ever to be taken, the final step in the downward process, by which the idea is carried out beyond specific differentiation to an individual embodiment. This last step he must take by a practical rather than by a theoretical activity, in his capacity as Nomethetes rather than as Philosophos, because the theoretical understanding is incapable of proceeding beyond the specific to the individual. The final step in the downward process is the foundation of a state.

These same two activities of negation and positing[3] are the spring of the Hegelian dialectic, but they, and the process which springs from them, are not for Hegel confined to the thinking of the philosopher, but are immanent in the being or idea which is his object.[4] He may, no doubt, retrace in thought the stages of the development of the idea, and it is the whole business of philosophy to do this; but he does not import the process which he follows,[5] and the idea is not dependent upon the co-operation of his theoretical insight for its development of its own implications. Nor does it need his co-operation in the practical capacity of a lawgiver even in order to take the final step from ideal being to real existence, as the law of an actual state.[6] The passage

---

[1] τὸ παντελῶς ὂν παντελῶς γνωστόν.

[2] νοητῶν ὄντων μετὰ ἀρχῆς.

[3] 'Aufheben' and 'Setzen' = ἀναιρεῖν and τιθέναι.

[4] The idea ('die absolute Idee') is thus still, like Plato's, eternal (since the process is a timeless one), but not, like Plato's, static.

[5] 'Dieser Entwickelung der Idee als eigener Tätigkeit ihrer Vernunft sieht das Denken als subjektives, ohne seinerseits eine Zutat hinzuzufügen, nur zu.' § 31 A.

[6] 'Die Idee [ist] nicht so ohnmächtig, um nur zu sollen, und nicht wirklich zu sein.' *Enzyklopädie*, § 5 A.

from ideal to real is itself only a later stage of that identical process of which the earlier stages consisted in the development of implications within the ideal itself, and the objectivity which the law of a state possesses is the product only of that same activity of affirming or 'positing' or *thesis* which is active also in the sphere of logic, as throughout the dialectical process.

It is this last point in the difference between the Hegelian and the Platonic doctrines which is specially relevant to our present purpose, because it gives to the state *as it exists in the world* a status in the scale of being which Plato was bound in consistency[1] to reserve for the idea 'laid up in heaven'. A realization or corporeal embodiment which was added to the idea extrinsically by the activity of a Nomothetes could not but diminish the perfection of its being, and an earthly state which was the product of such an embodiment, could not but be removed thereby from the sphere of those objects of which perfect knowledge is possible, or upon which the virtue of Sophia can be exercised. But it is the earthly state alone which is presented to the consciousness of the subject of it, and thus this metaphysical doctrine of Plato is discovered to be the ground of the political doctrine which we have already discussed,[2] by which the subject of the Polis is excluded from the exercise of Sophia. The subject must direct his conduct by reference to embodied standards, which are not proper objects of reason, but at most of 'right belief'; only the ruler, whose work it is to produce the embodiment, can direct his action by reference to the immaterial standards which reason can apprehend.

But since for Hegel the earthly realization of the state involves no admixture of the idea with an alien element,

---

[1] Though he finds it hard to be consistent on this point, cf. Ch. I, p. 27 *sup*.   [2] Ch. I, p. 28; Ch. II, p. 43 *sup*.

but is no less than the development of the idea itself, the earthly state possesses undiminished the status of being which Plato assigned to the idea, and the subjects for whom this earthly state is an object of knowledge are exercising in knowing it that Sophia, or knowledge of the highest kind, which Plato was bound to reserve to the philosopher;[1] in other words, it is because the idea is for Hegel dialectical in its nature that he is able to attribute to the subject the freedom which Plato confined to the ruler.

Sophia or insight in the subject *is* not, of course, ethical freedom, but only the condition of it. It is only a theoretical activity, whereas ethical freedom is a virtue of will. It realizes law only in the sense of knowing it, whereas law demands the further realization of being carried out in practice. The very objectivity which constitutes law a proper object of theoretical reason, incapacitates it for being, as such, a determinant of voluntary action. For this, a further activity in the subject is necessary in order to overcome this very objectivity; if it is a condition of *free* action that the law which determines it should be objective, it is

---

[1] Cf. on this point especially §§ 142–8, where, if we make the reservation throughout that Hegel is saying of the subject what Plato could say only of the ruler, the thought is wholly Platonic. The Platonic correlation of knowing and being is asserted in § 146: 'Die Substanz ist in diesem ihrem wirklichen Selbstbewußtsein sich wissend und damit Objekt des *Wissens*. Für das Subjekt haben die sittliche Substanz, ihre Gesetze und Gewalten einerseits als Gegenstand das Verhältnis, dass *sie sind*, im höchsten Sinne der Selbständigkeit' (my italics). And when Hegel continues in the next paragraph: 'Andererseits sind sie dem Subjekte nicht ein Fremdes, sondern es gibt das Zeugnis des Geistes von ihnen als von seinem eigenen Wesen, in welchem es sein Selbstgefühl hat, und darin als seinem von sich ununterschiedenen Elemente lebt,—ein Verhältnis, das unmittelbar, noch identischer als selbst Glauben und Zutrauen ist', we have the clearest echo of the Platonic doctrine that the philosopher 'loves what he knows' (see *Rep.* ii. 376a), because the reason which is object of knowledge is akin (οἰκεῖος, 'nicht ein Fremdes') to the reason in his soul by which he knows it.

FREEDOM IN THE STATE

a condition of free *action* that this objectivity should be overcome. To this end there must supervene upon the theoretical understanding an active response of the subject by which the objective law is so accepted and, as it were, spiritually digested, that it ceases any longer to be merely objective or over against the subject, and becomes a principle issuing in conduct from within. This supervening active response is for Hegel the essence of the practical element in morality; and this making inner of that which was outer, or was over against the subject as thinking, or the making subjective of what was objective, is the indispensable contribution of will to the realization of law as Sittlichkeit.

A somewhat analogous conversion is regarded by Aristotle as the end of the process of ethical education. In the beginning of the process his conduct must be prescribed to the pupil by an external authority; but he attains to ethical virtue only when he has absorbed into his own soul the principles by which the prescription was determined, so that they continue to inform his conduct no longer by dictation from without, but by animation from within. The analogy is not entirely accidental. The acquired disposition, or Hexis, which according to Aristotle is the internal spring of virtuous conduct, and at the same time the indispensable condition of the fulfilment of law,[1] is closely akin to the Hegelian ethical will. It differs from it in that it does not presuppose and supervene upon an insight into the rational necessity of the law. The externality which law possesses for the yet undischarged pupil of Aristotle's system does not consist in its objectivity to his theoretical understanding, but depends on the fact that its principles are ingrained in the soul only of his tutor or ruler, not yet in his own. It would be a closer analogy to say that Hegel's

[1] Cf. quotation, Ch. III, p. 96, n. *sup.*

ethical doctrine is like the superimposition of Aristotelian Ethics upon Kantian Morality. The insight of reason which is excluded from Aristotle's conception of ethical virtue becomes almost the whole of morality for Kant; almost, but not quite, because even for Kant the feeling of 'Respekt' must supervene upon the rational intuition of the moral law if it is to be carried out in conduct. Hegel's ethical will is the development of the germ just discernible in the Kantian 'Respekt' into something more like the Aristotelian Hexis.

There are two things to be observed about this conception of ethical will. In the first place, the law, like every object which is intelligible to thought, is universal, and therefore it belongs to the nature of the ethical will that it should *will the universal*. In order, that is to say, that it may enter into Sittlichkeit at all, will must have elevated itself above its natural condition, in which it is directed upon particular objects, to the level of thought, which can be by its nature directed only upon the universal.[1] The process of this elevation, or better 'conversion', is the process of moral education, and the essence of this process is the subjection of will to the discipline of thought.[2] The perfection of will, that is to say, which it achieves in becoming ethical, consists in its surrender of autonomy and its submission to the primacy of thought.[3]

---

[1] 'Der Intelligenz als denkend bleibt der Gegenstand und Inhalt *Allgemeines*, sie selbst verhält sich als allgemeine Tätigkeit,' § 13 A. Cf. 'Dass das Denken Allgemeines denkt, das Gefühl fühlt usw., sind lauter leere Tautologien'. *Vorlesungen über die Philosophie der Religion*, ed. Lasson, vol. i, p. 88.   [2] § 13, § 21; cf. § 258.

[3] There are passages in Hegel which seem to imply even more than this, namely that will, in order to become ethical, must surrender not only its autonomy, but its very identity as an activity distinct from thought. 'Im Willen beginnt ... die eigene Endlichkeit der Intelligenz, und nur dadurch, daß der Wille sich zum Denken wieder erhebt und seinen Zwecken die immanente Allgemeinheit gibt, hebt er den Unter-

In the second place, this will is only imperfectly differentiated from feeling. Hegel commonly speaks of it as 'will'; but the terms which he freely employs as synonymous with will are significant of the way in which he conceived it. These are 'Herz' (heart), 'Gesinnung' (sentiment or disposition) and, above all, the untranslatable 'Gemüt'.[1] 'Gemüt' is that in which the universal principle of reason is made 'inward', and so transformed from a theoretical to a potentially practical principle.

It is easy to see the affinity between Hegel's 'Gemüt' and the 'Thumoeides' which characterized Plato's auxiliaries,[2] and between Hegel's ethical will and the Andreia displayed in the absorption and active retention ('Soteria') of the form imposed by the law-giver,[3] which converts this from a form externally impressed, like a figure on the unresisting wax, into a principle of active information from within; or into what Aristotle was later to call a 'Hexis', or acquired disposition. There is in Plato the same subordination of the practical as auxiliary to the theoretical activity,[4] and the

schied der Form und des Inhalts auf und macht sich zum objektiven, unendlichen Willen'. § 13 A. 'Der Wille ist eine besondere Weise des Denkens; das Denken als sich übersetzend ins Dasein, als Trieb sich Dasein zu geben.' § 4 z. Cf. § 258 A, pp. 196–7.

[1] The same notion is present in 'Gemütlichkeit', though the reference of this term is rather to the conventions of social politeness than to the laws of ethical conduct. It may perhaps be rendered 'social good humour'. It is the opposite of frigidity, and is that which distinguishes an intimate social gathering from a formal one. In a company which is 'gemütlich' the conventions of politeness are not merely observed but *accepted*, so that polite actions are no longer performed in mechanical obedience to a rule, but as spontaneous expressions of good will.

[2] I suppose the analogy of the etymological derivation of these words is itself not accidental. 'Gemüt' is clearly connected with 'Mut' as 'Thumoeides' is with '$\theta\bar{v}\mu os$', and 'Mut' means $\theta\bar{v}\mu os$.

[3] Cf. Ch. III, p. 94 *sup*.

[4] $\tau\hat{\omega}$ $\lambda o\gamma\iota\sigma\tau\iota\kappa\hat{\omega}$ $\check{a}\rho\chi\epsilon\iota\nu$ $\pi\rho o\sigma\acute{\eta}\kappa\epsilon\iota$. This hegemony of reason is involved in the whole analogy of the guardians' activity with $\tau\acute{\epsilon}\chi\nu\eta$.

same consequent failure to conceive will as anything distinct both from reason and desire.[1]

The importance of these affinities can hardly be overrated. All the deficiencies which have always been felt in Hegel's doctrine of ethical will depend upon the fact that he has not wholly transcended the Platonic standpoint, and that although he possesses, what Plato lacked, a name for will, he means by it so little more than Plato meant by To Thumoeides.

Hegel's conception of ethical freedom involves the union in the same individual of the two faculties of To Logistikon and To Thumoeides which Plato had conceived in separation as residing the one in the ruler as tutor, the other in the auxiliary as pupil; it involves, further, the extension to all members of society of the virtue which Plato had confined to the guardians, so that a man needs the same qualification to make him a subject in the State as to make him a ruler in the Polis. In both of these respects Hegel has transcended Plato. The deficiency at which we have hinted consists in this, that although Hegel has endowed his subjects with all the virtue that the Platonic guardian possessed, he has not done more; he has not endowed them with a faculty which the Platonic guardian himself did not possess, namely with an autonomous faculty of will.

Hegel was enabled to overcome the limitations of the Platonic political philosophy by the measure in which he transcended the Platonic metaphysics;[2] we shall endeavour to show later that the deficiency of his political philosophy was due to an insufficiency in that transcendence.[3] But we have to turn first to consider the second meaning in which Hegel uses the term 'subjective freedom'.

---

[1] It is notorious that the conception, and the very name, of will was lacking to Greek ethics.
[2] Cf. pp. 121 ff. *sup.*
[3] pp. 135 ff. *inf.*

II

As the objectivity of law is the condition of one freedom, so its generality is the condition of another. The particular detail of action which no general regulation can determine is left to the free choice[1] of the subject, and it is essential to the securing of this freedom of choice that the law should be neither so particularized nor capable of such particularization as would enable it to prescribe to the individual a specific performance.

Hegel regards it as distinctively characteristic of the modern state that the determination of its law should stop short at the general and leave a scope for the undetermined choice of the subject in the particular means of its fulfilment.[2] Thus the demands of the state upon the services of its citizens must be demands for money,[3] not for specific performances[4] or for contributions in kind. In levying a monetary tax the state is restricting itself to prescribing the general value of the contribution which it requires and leaving the determination of its particular nature, or of the particular manner of its earning, to the choice of the individual.[5] It is essential, again, to any state that it should be organized, that is to say that its individual members should be distributed in classes, professions, and trades; but it is typical of the modern state that the law renounces control of the particular distribution. Whereas in Plato's Polis it had been a task for the rulers to assign to each one of their subjects a particular sphere or trade, in the State the choice of trade or profession is left to the individual.[6]

The exercise of this choice by the citizen is clearly a subjective activity, since it is by definition a choice not deter-

---

[1] 'Willkür.' For what follows, cf. more in detail Appendix E, p. 101 *sup*. [2] Vorrede, p. 14. [3] Taxation.
[4] Such as λειτουργίαι. [5] § 299. [6] § 206.

mined by the system of law presented as object to the understanding. It is a condition of the possibility of this activity that the law should be limited in the scope of its determination, and it might seem that the law suffered by this limitation *merely* a diminution in the sphere of its authority; that it was constrained to admit a sphere of lawlessness and arbitrary choice like a kind of Alsatia within its bounds, as a prudent ruler might find himself obliged to sacrifice a portion of his territory in order to confirm his hold upon the remainder. But this is not so, for the exercise of this undetermined choice issues in fact in the fulfilment of the law and is the indispensable means of its realization. A subject may choose freely[1] to make shoes or to tend cattle; his choice between these alternatives is not determined by his obligation to obey the law and is to be derived from no necessity of reason, but simply from his desire to satisfy his economic wants. Nevertheless, by his choice he does give reality to what is a necessity of reason,[2] namely the general design that the community should be organized in trades; and the general law that a certain proportion of wealth should be contributed in taxation, depends for the possibility of its fulfilment upon this choice of a particular means of production.

That scope should be left for an activity in the subject undetermined by the law is thus the condition not only of the freedom of the subject,[3] but of the actualization of the law itself.[4]

---

[1] No doubt his choice is determined often enough by economic necessity, but it is free in the sense that it is quite unconstrained by law.   [2] § 206.

[3] 'Die Anerkennung und das Recht, daß, *was* in der bürgerlichen Gesellschaft und im Staate *durch die Vernunft notwendig ist, zugleich durch die Willkür vermittelt geschehe*, ist die nähere Bestimmung dessen, was vornehmlich in der allgemeinen Vorstellung Freiheit heißt.' § 206 A (my italics).

[4] 'Neque enim lex impletur nisi libero arbitrio.' A comparison of

In this doctrine Hegel is maintaining, as before, that a subjective practical activity, or an activity of will, is essential to the realization of the State; that the freedom of the subject consists in this activity; that the State differs from the Polis mainly in securing this freedom and the Hegelian from the Platonic philosophy mainly in recognizing it both as a right of the subject and as a condition of the fulfilment of law.

It is unnecessary to repeat what has been shown already,[1] that this doctrine, although it is capable of expression in an almost identical phraseology with the doctrine of ethical will which we considered earlier in this chapter, is entirely different from it.

This latter activity we have called the economic will. It is a conception of will alternative to, but in itself no more adequate than, Hegel's conception of the ethical will. Like the ethical will, it bears on itself all the marks of its Platonic origin. As the former conception failed of adequacy by being imperfectly differentiated from reason, so the latter fails by being imperfectly differentiated from desire.[2]

The failure of Greek ethics to achieve a notion of will was a necessary consequence of Greek metaphysics. The essence of this metaphysics was the distinction within the universe of an intelligible nature from a sensible nature,

these words of St. Augustine with those of Aristotle quoted above (p. 96, n.) provides an illustration of the difference between Law and Nomos in this respect. Nomos requires for its fulfilment 'Ethos' in the subject; but Law free will.

[1] Ch. III, pp. 80 ff., *sup.*; App. E., p. 101.

[2] I do not of course mean that the two alternative conceptions included under Hegel's 'Wille' represent no advance upon anything in Plato. The very use of the term 'will', to go no further, represents an advance. But I do mean that Hegel's thinking lags behind his terminology.

the former being the ground, or *ratio essendi*, of the latter.[1] The ground of sensible nature is, in other words, itself a *nature*.

In such a universe there is no room for will. Nature may be the object of knowledge on the one hand and of appetition on the other; but not of a third activity distinct from either. Thus sensible nature may be the object either of sensuous perception or of sensuous desire, intelligible nature either of theoretical understanding or of non-sensuous appetition. Desire and appetition are, of course, not theoretical activities; nature is not confined to being object of knowledge, it can also move to practical activity, but it can move only as end or final cause. Hence practical activity is confined to appetition or direction upon an end, whether it is appetition for a sensible, and therefore particular, or for an intelligible, and therefore universal object.

Hegel's metaphysical doctrine of the State bears a resemblance, which is not accidental, to the Platonic metaphysic of nature. The world of historical appearance—the constitutions, bodies of custom and historical systems of law presented to the consciousness of the subject in an actual State—he conceived as a 'second nature'.[2] Within this world he makes a distinction between the 'idea' and its historical manifestation precisely analogous to the Platonic distinction between the intelligible and the sensible within the world of physical nature.[3] States as historical existences

[1] Whether or not Plato was guilty of χωρισμός, that is to say whether he so misconceived this distinction that he misconstrued the twofold nature of the universe as a duplication of universes, is a question which is not relevant here. If he was, his philosophy was differentiated thereby from Aristotle's, but we are concerned to point out a characteristic which his philosophy has in common with Aristotle's, and I suppose also with Greek philosophy in general. At least I shall use 'Greek philosophy' as a compendious term to designate what I take to be common to Plato and Aristotle. [2] § 4. [3] § 1.

FREEDOM IN THE STATE

appearing in time and localized in place are objects of an inferior kind of knowledge, namely of the empirical sciences of history or positive jurisprudence;[1] but within this historical world reason can discern an intelligible core, which is related to the merely historical as essence to appearance,[2] and is thus the ground at once of its being and of its being understood. This core is the total system of universal determinations which can be developed out of the concept by the dialectic of reason; it is what Hegel calls the 'idea' of the State, and is the proper object of a Philosophy of Right.[3] This 'idea' of the State is thus conceived under the categories proper to an intelligible nature; it is the object of the highest kind of knowing, namely of philosophical reason, and is possessed of the highest degree of being.[4] It is related, in a word, to the world of historical appearance as intelligible nature to sensible; it is completely, as the phenomenal is only partially, both real and knowable. If the historical world in which the conduct of the subject has to take place is exhausted in this dichotomy, it is clear that there is nothing in it which can properly be object to his will. The 'idea' or essence of the State may be object to his reason, and in the indeterminacy of its accidents he may find scope for the satisfaction of desire. He may thus unite in himself the two activities which Plato distributed among two classes in his Polis, assigning reason to the ruler and desire to the subject; but he cannot be conceived to exercise an activity radically distinct from either.

There is the strictest reciprocal implication between the psychology of human nature and the metaphysics of law. Thus the recognition of a positive element as essential to

[1] § 3, § 212 A, § 258 A, pp. 196–8.
[2] See especially Vorrede, pp. 14–15; and § 3.
[3] § 1. [4] § 146.

law involves the recognition of a faculty of will as essential to man, and vice versa. The implication is illustrated in Plato's own doctrine; the law to which the auxiliary class is submitted is positive in the sense that it is opaque to *their* intelligence, and consequently this class develops in its obedience to it that Andreia which is Plato's nearest anticipation of a virtue of will. But this positivity does not for Plato belong to the nature of law. The nature of law is to be wholly reasonable, and it is positive only in so far as it is obscurely apprehended. The same enlightenment of the understanding which removes the positive element from law, raises the subject above the stage at which a virtue of will needs to be exercised in obeying it.[1] Will is not essential to his nature, but depends upon a defect of his understanding, just as the positivity of law is only an appearance, depending on the obscurity with which it is apprehended. But if the essence of law is held to consist in its imperative character, if, that is to say, law is constituted law in virtue of an element superadded to its nature as an intelligible statement, then there must be recognized a faculty of will as an essential element in the nature of man, being subject to such a law. This imperative element can operate upon the subject as object neither of his understanding nor of his desire, since only what *is* in some sense of the word can be object of either of these, whereas it is the essence of the imperative that it is not, but ought to be.

If we have an original conviction that will belongs to the essence of human nature, that may serve as a ground for the rejection of a metaphysics which would involve the elimination of will from the conception of moral activity. It is characteristic of the attitude of mind which we call Common Sense that it argues from that conviction to this conclusion; and some such argument is implicit in the ordinary

[1] See Ch. II, p. 66 *sup.*

reaction of the unsophisticated moral man against the metaphysical foundation of Hegelian Ethics.[1] The implication holds equally in the reverse direction; if we could have such an insight into the ground of moral rules as would assure us that an imperative character was essential to them, we could conclude from this premiss that will is an essential element of human nature. It is the distinguishing characteristic of Common Sense reasoning that it proceeds always in the former direction, never in the latter. Its immediate certainty is the psychological, not the metaphysical one. But it is the error of Common Sense philosophy that it assumes this certainty to be a natural endowment of the species man and a universal and permanent possession of human nature. It commonly ignores the paradox which this assumption involves, namely that men should have begun so late in history to employ a faculty which *ex hypothesi* they possessed from the earliest times. The Greek was not aware of that faculty which we call will. Was this ignorance due simply to his omission to reflect on his own nature? Had he but to 'look within himself', in Locke's phrase, in order to perceive it, and was his failure due merely to the misdirection of his gaze? That man possessed the faculty of Common Sense two thousand years before he exercised it is an assertion which it is charitable to call a paradox because it is a meaningless assertion. Yet this is the paradox, or the nonsense, to which a philosophy of Common Sense is committed.

The truth is that the common-sense convictions which form part of the intellectual heritage of the modern world were acquired and formed under the long discipline of Christian faith, and that the Greeks did not possess them because they had not been educated in Christian doctrine.

[1] Cf. the method adopted by G. E. Moore in *Principia Ethica*, of showing that the founding of ethics upon ontology is inconsistent with the convictions of Common Sense about moral activity.

It would be out of place to elaborate this thesis in general here and I must refer to what I have written elsewhere for confirmation both of it and of much else of what follows in this chapter;[1] but the logical connexion between Christian doctrine and the particular common-sense conviction that will is a part of human nature becomes clearer if we recognize that metaphysics forms a middle term between religious dogma and common sense. The doctrine that a positive element is essential to law implies a faculty of will in man, and is implied in its turn by the doctrine that the supreme law for man is the command of God, that is to say that it belongs to its essence to issue from God's *will*. If we ask now for the source of that doctrine which attributes will to God, there can be no doubt about the answer; it is the revelation embodied in the Old Testament.

The doctrines that God created the world, that he rules human affairs as Providence, that he issues commands to men and punishes transgressions: all these imply a conception of an activity of will in God which is conspicuously absent from any[2] Greek theology. These are also, through the channels which I have indicated, the ultimate sources of those elements in the convictions of Common Sense which were absent from the Greek consciousness. Thus it comes about that, profoundly different as are the approaches to metaphysics from Common Sense on the one hand and from the authority of revelation on the other, the goal of both is the same. A Greek ontology (or Rationalism) is

[1] 'The Christian Doctrine of Creation and the Rise of Modern Natural Science' in *Mind*, Oct. 1934; 'The opposition between Hegel and the Philosophy of Empiricism', in *Verhandlungen des dritten Hegel-Kongresses*, Tübingen and Haarlem, 1934.

[2] Plato's conception of the divine Demiurge in the *Timaeus* forms an exception to this statement; it is one of the points at which an anticipation of Christian doctrine is found in Plato. But there is still a vitally important difference between the two conceptions of Demiurge and of Creator, for which I must refer to Ch. VI *inf.*

FREEDOM IN THE STATE

obnoxious to the criticisms of Common Sense in virtue of the same characteristics which exposed it in an earlier age to the assaults of Christian orthodoxy.

The defect of Hegel's metaphysics, by which he is prevented from attributing to will its true place as an element of human nature, is due likewise to his failure to absorb into his philosophy the truth of the Old Testament doctrine of law; namely that law has its source in will. It is due to his denial of what that doctrine implies; that law is positive in its essential nature.

The two correlative defects of Hegel's philosophy, his failure to recognize the voluntary activity of man and the positive character of law, may thus be referred for their ultimate source to his failure to assimilate in its fullness the Christian doctrine of God. But Hegel would not have been a great philosopher if he had been a Rationalist pure and simple. So far is his philosophy from being the revival of an undiluted Platonism that we have been able to employ the contrast with Plato to exhibit its most distinctive characteristics. If it is the defect of Hegel's psychology that he fails to recognize the peculiar nature of will as the subjective spring of activity, so that, although he employs the term 'Wille', he employs it interchangeably with the terms 'Herz', 'Gemüt', and 'Geist', and can even be betrayed upon occasion into speaking of will as 'eine besondere Weise des Denkens',[1] it is still a vast advance upon Plato that he should maintain that the perfection of human action depends upon the presence, not upon the elimination, of this subjective element. This is what is implied in the substitution of Freedom for Justice as the universal human virtue. If, again, it is the defect of Hegel's theory of law, that he fails to recognize that it belongs to the essence of law to be positive,[2] still he differentiates law very sharply from Nomos by the

[1] See p. 126, n. 3, *sup*.   [2] 'positiv.'

doctrine, upon which he strongly insists, that it belongs to the essence of law to be 'posited'.[1] Law contains no element not derived from the 'idea' which is the object of speculative reason, but the activity of 'positing', or of thesis, is inherent in the idea itself in virtue of its nature as dialectical. Thus Hegel's doctrine of Law, like his doctrine of Freedom,[2] is dependent upon his metaphysical doctrine of the Dialectic.

We may conclude this chapter by pointing out that these un-Platonic elements in Hegel are themselves derived from a source in Christian revelation. If Hegel's defects are due to his failure to absorb the truth of this revelation in its completeness, the positive achievement by which he is enabled to surpass Plato is due to the fact that he has still not left it unabsorbed. It is possible indeed to specify more precisely which elements of Christianity Hegel has assimilated and which he has ignored: he has on the whole ignored the revelation of the Old Testament but assimilated the revelation of the New. His philosophy shows no trace of the metaphysics of will implicit in the Judaic doctrines of the Creation and the Law, which entails the recognition that contingency is essential to nature,[3] positivity to law, and will to the perfection of man; but he is steeped in the Christian teachings of the Trinity, the Incarnation and Redemption, and the whole of his thought is pervaded by their implications.[4] These doctrines are the source of those elements in Hegel's philosophy which differentiate it most markedly from Plato's.

We have observed the dependence both of the Hegelian philosophy of law and the Hegelian doctrine of freedom upon the metaphysical doctrine that the Idea is dialectical.

---

[1] 'gesetzt', see p. 119 *sup*.
[2] Cf. p. 124 *sup*.
[3] Cf. the article in *Mind* referred to above, p. 136, n. 1.
[4] 'Für Hegel ist die christliche Erlösungsvorstellung die spekulativ massgebliche'. R. Kroner, *Von Kant bis Hegel*, vol. ii, p. 236.

Hegel himself insists throughout his writings that the truth which receives its philosophical expression in the Dialectic is the same truth which is expressed in the form of religious imagery in the Christian doctrine of the Trinity.[1] This doctrine exceeds anything to be found in any[2] Greek theology by its attribution to God of a power of efficient causation. Plato's Idea of the Good is the object only, not the subject of any activity; Aristotle's God is, indeed, the subject of activity, but of an activity purely theoretical, and terminating upon himself. When Hegel sums up his metaphysics by saying (with a side-glance at Spinoza) that he conceives the Absolute not as Substance but as Subject, he is only attributing to it that power of imparting self in the production of another which the doctrine of the Trinity

[1] I should add here to avoid misunderstanding that I do not accept Hegel's own theory of the relation between philosophy and religion, nor consequently his conception of the relation of his own philosophy to the Christian revelation. For Hegel the religious imagination ('Vorstellung') is related to the philosophical concept somewhat in the manner in which the visible illustration of a triangle, e.g., is related to the mathematical concept of it. It is an indispensable stage in the progress of the mind towards the concept, but a stage which is transcended when the concept has been reached. The conclusions of the philosopher are dependent upon none but logical evidence, and it follows that the opacity to reason characteristic of a revealed truth is not essential to the truth revealed but adheres to it only in so far as it is imperfectly understood. Hegel's Rationalism thus shows itself in his theory of revealed religion in the same way as in his theories of law and of will. As in those theories the elements of positivity in law and of will in human action were found to depend in the last analysis upon deficiency of reason; so in this theory the element of revelation in truth. But here also Hegel's theory is something less than Christian; it does not contain the belief that the word of God is true because God has uttered it, but only the very different one that God has uttered it because it is true. And here also his doctrine has closer affinities to the teaching of the New Testament than to that of the Old; it involves a conception of the Word of God nearer to that of the fourth Gospel than to that of the Hebrew prophets.

[2] The theology of the *Timaeus* is again an exception; cf. p. 136, n. 2, *sup.*

ascribes to God. But the doctrine of the Trinity does not exhaust the Christian revelation of God. To conceive the causality of God to extend no farther than to the generation of the Son, is to ignore the doctrine of the Creation,[1] in which there is attributed to God an activity radically different from that of generation in that it is a pure activity of will.

To elaborate in detail the twofold thesis: that Hegel's philosophy is enabled to surpass Plato's by its absorption of the truths of the Christian revelation, but that at the same time this absorption is insufficient and incomplete, is a task far beyond the scope of this work, but I may avoid misunderstanding by adding two remarks in conclusion of this chapter.

It may seem that it is Hegel's appropriation of Christian doctrines which is responsible for that fantastic or mystical or 'metaphysical' element in his philosophy which common sense finds shocking. This is not true. I do not of course deny the presence of that element, but I assert that it is due in every instance not to his assimilation of Christian doctrines, but to the insufficiency of the assimilation. Those philosophies which present the firmest opposition to this tendency in Hegel, e.g. the common-sense Empiricism in one respect, the moral philosophy of Kant in another, are enabled to do so because (whatever their narrowness in other regards) they are more, not less, firmly based upon at least one Christian doctrine which is not fully assimilated in the philosophy of Hegel, Locke, e.g., upon the doctrine of Creation, Kant on that of the Law. Their opposition to Hegel is waged in the name of *Christiana sanitas*.

---

[1] Hegel habitually confuses the generation of the Son with the Creation of the world. For instances see my paper on Hegel and Empiricism, cited above, p. 136, n. 1.

FREEDOM IN THE STATE

It may be thought further that to attribute the advance of Hegel over Plato to the influence of Christian ideas is incompatible with the thesis maintained in the earlier part of this book, that Hegel surpasses Plato by developing the consequences implicit in the Platonic philosophy itself. But these two theses are not really incompatible. It is an old story that Plato contains anticipations of Christian doctrine, and it is precisely these implications which are further developed in the philosophy of Hegel. The Christian revelation is not a body of doctrine alien to truth; it contains truths which, when elicited from it by the work of thought, can be perceived in some cases to be the proper conclusion of the development begun in Greek speculation. But I must add my conviction that although such conclusions may be understood *ex post facto* to be the proper consummation of pre-Christian philosophy, they could not have been attained by the work of unaided reason upon pre-Christian premisses.

V

'CIVIL SOCIETY' AND STATE IN HEGEL

WE may see the first faint anticipation of the distinction between 'society' and State in Plato's distinction between the 'first city' and the ideal Polis. We have distinguished the 'first city' as an economic from the ideal Polis as a political society, but that terminology rests upon the discovery of a far more radical difference between them than any which Plato recognized. It implies that political differs from economic society in the kind of law proper to it; whereas Plato recognized no difference between the form realized in the 'first city' and that realized in the ideal Polis, but only between the manner of its realization in each. The law imposed by the ruler was not *super*-imposed upon a society possessing already a law of its own; it was the same law which constituted the original society a society at all, only re-imposed.

Law, on Plato's theory, is the form of society, as economic activity is its matter. Since matter has no real existence without form, to deny that economic activity has its proper laws is to deny a real existence to economic society. Plato's account of the 'coming to be' of the city, in which the first city is represented as earlier in time than the second, does not imply the ascription of real existence to an economic apart from a political society. It is not history, but Muthos; and the doctrine of the relation of the economic to the political which it is intended to convey is presented later in the *Republic* in terms adequate to Logos, when the society of the 'first city' is incorporated as the 'third class' within the ideal Polis and it becomes clear that its relation to the law imposed by the rulers is that of matter to form. The Platonic teaching is thus that economic activity and political

'CIVIL SOCIETY' AND STATE IN HEGEL 143

order are distinguishable in thought, but not separable in actuality. Each is a potency realized only in union with the other, and the unity of the Polis depends upon this reciprocal dependence of its two elements. It was as essential to Plato's conception of the unity of the Polis that there should be no economic laws as it was to the Aristotelian conception of physical nature that there should be no laws of matter.[1]

The revolution of thought at the end of the Middle Ages which founded the modern science of nature and discredited the Aristotelian philosophy was based upon the two principles that there are laws of matter, and that matter is a substance; i.e. that it is not merely distinguishable from form in thought, but that it has a real being apart from form.[2] These two propositions necessitate one another reciprocally, and we need not stay to inquire which, if either, is prior to the other as ground to consequent.

In the realm of political philosophy a similar revolution found expression in the doctrine of a State of Nature.[3] The State of Nature was the original condition of man, upon which the form of political society had been imposed. To this extent it corresponded to Plato's conception of economic society as matter awaiting the imposition of form. What was new and quite un-Platonic in the doctrine of the State of Nature was the conception that this state was subject to laws of its own different in kind from those later

---

[1] e.g. no laws of the communication of motion valid for all material objects irrespective of their kind.

[2] The further consequence was drawn that form is an extrinsic denomination imposed upon the material substance by the imperfection of the perceiving mind; as by Spinoza in his doctrine that species are *modi cogitandi*, and by Locke in his doctrine that they are 'nominal essences'.

[3] I have no doubt that I am egregiously post-dating both 'revolutions', and that both doctrines have their roots far back in the Middle Ages, and earlier. But I must begin where my knowledge begins: in political philosophy, with Hobbes.

144 'CIVIL SOCIETY' AND STATE IN HEGEL

imposed by government, with the implication that the State of Nature was not merely distinguishable in thought from the political order to which it was submitted, but that it had a substantial being independently of it. This independence was expressed by the ascription of a real existence to the State of Nature temporally prior to the foundation of the political state, as the contemporary philosophies of nature expressed the independence of matter by representing it as spatially separate from the mind (it was supposed to act upon mind causally). No doubt these figures of temporal priority and spatial externality are inadequate expressions of the truth which their authors are groping after. But to discount them altogether and to say, e.g. of Hobbes, that his historical sequence is only a childish metaphor for logical priority, and that when he makes a temporal distinction between the natural and the political state, this is only a clumsy expression of what Plato had expressed adequately by distinguishing but not separating the form and matter of the state—all this is to make out that the originality of Hobbes depends solely on his not having understood Aristotle. As if λόγῳ πρότερον and *distinctio rationis* had not been commonplaces of the learned world for centuries! Hobbes's historical sequence of states is undoubtedly a clumsy expression, but of something which had *not* been expressed in Greek political philosophy; just as the conception of material substance as spatially separated from the mind was the no less crude expression of a truth not contained in the Greek philosophy of nature. Mythological as the Hobbesian account may still appear, it is not, as Plato's story of the 'first city' is, mere Muthos. The historical sequence which it asserts is not a mere accident of allegorical clothing.[1]

---

[1] The difference may perhaps be expressed by saying that whereas Plato's 'first city' is simply imagined, Hobbes's State of Nature is imagined as past. A similar temporal reference creeps into the

That is to say the truth which it is an endeavour to express is not exhausted if the temporal discrimination of the two states is interpreted merely as a metaphor for a logical distinction.

I have spoken hitherto as though economic laws were the only laws which prevailed in the State of Nature, but this is an over-simplification. 'Natural Law' is an ambiguous term, including not one only, but two different meanings, which were usually not distinguished by those who used it most. Its ambiguity depends in the last resort upon a failure to determine precisely what is 'natural' in man, his passions or his reason. It was found impossible either to reconcile these two conceptions, or to discard either of them completely in favour of the other. Hence the State of Nature means not one but at the same time both of two things: the state in which man's action is determined by his passions and the state in which man's action is determined by his reason. Laws of nature have accordingly a double meaning also: they are laws of the passions and laws of reason. This duplicity does not extend only to the denotation but also to the very meaning of the term. What both laws have in common and what distinguishes both equally from positive law is that they have their source in no will. Both equally may be called laws of reason, but each in a different sense: the one in the sense of being a law discerned by reason in the working of the passions, the other in the sense of being prescribed by reason to the passions.[1] Both

Utopias of this period. They are conceptions not of an ideal 'laid up in heaven' and therefore timeless, but imagined to have an existence dated in the present on an undiscovered portion of the earth's surface. When this device is discarded, the temporal reference remains, but is transferred to the future. The Utopia becomes a prophecy and the ideal a millennium.

[1] When Cobbett, e.g., defines the law of nature as 'the law of self-preservation and self-enjoyment, without any restraint imposed by a regard for the good of our neighbours', he is using the term in the

equally may be termed universal, but the one in the sense of being universally operative, the other in the sense of being universally valid. The one is a law of conduct which, though it is capable of being understood, determines conduct equally whether it is understood or not; the other is a law which by its very nature can determine conduct only in so far as it is understood, so that conduct must be said in strictness to be determined not by the law but by the conception of it.

Thus the State of Nature was conceived as subject at once to two different kinds of laws, (i) to the laws of the passions, which I have termed 'economic' laws, by an anticipation of that into which they were to develop later, and (ii) to the laws prescribed to reason, which I will distinguish henceforth by a similar licence under the name of Civil Law.[1]

No philosopher could conceive the State of Nature as a state in which either kind of law prevailed to the entire

former sense. An example of a law of nature in the latter sense is the law that every man shall respect in all other rational creatures the same rights which he claims for himself.

[1] The use of this term is open to some objection and I employ it only in default of a better. It has the advantage that it indicates the historical derivation of this conception of Natural Law from Roman Law ('Jus Gentium', 'Jus Naturae'), and the derivation from it of Hegel's 'abstraktes Recht'; but the disadvantage that it obscures the fact that the Kantian Moral Law was directly derived from it also.

There is the further inconvenience that I am using to designate a kind of natural law the very term which was used as its opposite by some of the early political philosophers who recognized no other distinction than that simple one of the social from the pre-social state. But this inconvenience is inevitable. When the further distinction came to be drawn between society and State, and 'natural law' developed into the conception of a law which was social without being positive, then the twofold nature of this law became explicit in the distinction between economic and civil law. I am trying to mark the germ of this distinction in the conception of natural law in which it was not explicit, and have no resource but to differentiate the two notions concealed together in it by terms properly applicable only to what was later developed from them.

'CIVIL SOCIETY' AND STATE IN HEGEL 147

exclusion of the other, but the dividing line between the two great traditions of modern philosophy, the Empiricist and the Rationalist,[1] is to be drawn in the sphere of political theory according as the one sense of natural law predominates over the other.

I shall consider the development of the idea of natural law in each of these traditions separately, and in the Empiricist first.

(i) Although Hobbes admitted that there were laws of nature, he almost nullified the admission by maintaining that in the State of Nature they are necessarily inoperative and void. For this reason they had no validity after the contract and could in no way limit the scope of the law of the State. Thus Hobbes does not distinguish the State from society, nor the scope of political regulation from that of a law which should be social without being positive. But in ascribing to the pre-social state at least the potentialities of law, he presents the germ from which the distinction could grow.

The distinction is developed in Locke. Locke takes the laws of nature far more seriously than Hobbes had done. He is unwilling to regard them as wholly inoperative even in the State of Nature, and is *therefore* able to claim for them a continued operation 'after the contract', and to regard them as limiting the scope of positive enactment within society itself. The distinction between positive and 'natural' law is thus no longer simply co-terminous with that between the social and pre-social states, but reappears within the social state itself as that between the State and 'society'.

If we continue to confine ourselves to the one significa-

[1] I shall use the terms 'Empiricism' and 'Rationalism' throughout this chapter in the special and limited sense in which they designate these two traditions of modern European philosophy.

tion of natural law, then this 'society' which is distinguished from the State must be determined as economic society, and the laws by which it is governed as economic laws. There is a genuine sense in which these laws are natural, and in which they may be held to set at once a limit and an end to legislative activity. Legislation is limited in its scope by the condition that it must refrain from interference with the working of economic laws within the economic sphere. It must not, e.g., draft particular individuals into particular industries, but must content itself with preserving a general order, within which the distribution of particular employments may be determined by that individual choice which is free in the sense that it is determined only by economic necessity. It must not levy contributions of goods or services, but must confine itself to the imposition of monetary taxes, leaving the particular work to be done by the subject to be determined by the economic laws which can operate at all only in so far as his choice is free. To secure these limitations was one of the great aims of the English Liberalism which derived its principles from Locke; and they are clearly identical with the condition of generality in the law, which Hegel regarded as essential to the freedom of (economic) will in the subject.[1]

The integrity of person, property, and contract are the main conditions of this liberty, since these are barriers for the preservation of a sphere of conduct against the intrusion of any determinant save a man's own desires. It is only when desires are allowed to operate in such freedom from interference that economic activity can exhibit its proper form of lawfulness.

But in an economic society so conceived, economic laws cannot be the only laws which are operative. Person,

[1] Ch. IV, pp. 129 ff., *sup*.

'CIVIL SOCIETY' AND STATE IN HEGEL 149

property, and contract are preserved *for* the free development of economic activity into a system regulated by economic laws; but they are preserved *by* a system of laws which are not economic at all, but civil, and this latter law is differentiated from the former once for all by the crucial test, that it always belongs to the nature of the latter that it can operate only in so far as it is understood, whereas economic laws operate equally whether they are understood or not.

Thus an Empiricist philosophy cannot exclude civil law from its conception of society; but it degrades it to the status of a means to the securing of economic freedom.

(ii) This system of civil law forms the essence of the Rationalist conception of society, but it is characteristic of Rationalism to regard the realization of it as an end in itself, not desirable simply as a means to economic satisfaction. The system has its claim upon the acceptance of a reasonable being because it is itself reasonable, that is to say deducible *a priori* from self-evident principles; and the subject is free in accepting it because his reason is submitted to no alien force but only to reason. No doubt, since this law terminates in the maintenance of a system of private property, it must be admitted that there is scope within the barriers thus erected for the exercise of an activity which is free in the quite different sense that it is determined by desire, and it is compatible with the Rationalist view of society to recognize that this activity itself exhibits laws in its working which cannot indeed be deduced *a priori* by reason, but which are capable of being established *a posteriori*. What is characteristic of Rationalism is that it reverses the order of priority conceived by Empiricism to hold between the two freedoms and the two laws. A genuine reconciliation of the conflicting claims would have been possible only upon the basis of the recognition of their difference; and this neither school attained. Each identified freedom with its own special conception of it and thus could not recognize the alternative conception as a form of freedom at all.

This law is clearly capable of a development similar to the former, from being conceived as a law of the State of Nature merely, to being conceived as a law of society which can constitute both an end and a limit to the authority of positive law.

This system of civil law is what Hegel calls 'abstract right' ('das abstrakte Recht'), and it is for Hegel, as for his Rationalist predecessors, reasonable or natural in the sense that it is systematically deducible[1] by reason from the speculative concept of freedom. This concept is itself developed by reason through the dialectical process which begins in the 'Logic'; so that the determinations of the system of right have a *logical* necessity not inferior to that of any thesis within the sphere of Logic itself. It thus possesses that character of being pervious to the understanding of the reasonable subject which is for Hegel the essential condition of (ethical)[2] freedom.

The sphere in the realm of 'Sittlichkeit' which Hegel distinguishes from the State as 'bürgerliche Gesellschaft'[3] combines in itself (and we must add, confuses) *both* the determinations by which we have found it possible to differentiate 'society' from State. It is both economic society and civil society; it is the sphere in which both economic laws are fulfilled and civil law is enforced.[4]

---

[1] The first of the three main divisions of the *Philosophie des Rechts* is occupied with this deduction (§§ 34–103).
[2] I shall use this term throughout the present chapter in the sense defined above, Ch. IV, p. 110 *sup*.   [3] §§ 182–56.
[4] Thus the first of the three main headings under which Hegel treats 'bürgerliche Gesellschaft' is 'Das System der Bedürfnisse' (§§ 189–208), the second 'Die Rechtspflege' (§ 209–29).

'CIVIL SOCIETY' AND STATE IN HEGEL 151

Thus while Hobbes and Plato fail, each for an opposite reason, to distinguish 'society' from State, Hobbes because he denied that natural law could operate within society, Plato because he denied that any laws other than natural could be valid within the State, Hegel develops the principle, implicit in Locke, of a demarcation of spheres. There must be a sphere of natural law within the state; although a state is not a State unless there is also another sphere in which this is 'transcended'.

But 'bürgerliche Gesellschaft' is really constituted what it is by the operation within it of two sorts of law, each 'natural' in a different sense of the word, and each qualified further to serve as a condition of freedom in the subject in a different sense of that word,[1] and Hegel never clearly distinguishes between these two kinds of law, as he does not distinguish between the two kinds of freedom of which they are conditions. This failure is, I suggest, the main cause of the extreme difficulty which faces any attempt to elucidate Hegel's doctrine of the relation of 'society' to 'State', and of the manner in which the former is 'transcended' in the latter.

I do not believe that it is possible to find in Hegel or to construe out of his words a single consistent doctrine of the relation of 'bürgerliche Gesellschaft' to 'Staat', or a single consistent account of the 'transition' from the one to the other. There are to be found in him on the contrary two different lines of argument, not really consistent with one another. These I shall distinguish under the names of the 'Rationalist' and the 'Platonic' respectively, and I shall endeavour in my exposition to follow each separately and the former first.

---

[1] It is *because* the laws which condition them are in one sense or another 'natural', that the freedom which they make possible in the subject is a freedom either of reason or of desire ('ethical' or 'economic' freedom), but not of will.

(i) Hegel's doctrine is, indeed, not difficult to state in general terms. The State is the highest stage in the realization of the idea of 'Sittlichkeit'. 'Bürgerliche Gesellschaft' is a lower stage in the same process, and thought is necessitated to make the transition from the lower to the higher insomuch as 'bürgerliche Gesellschaft' exhibits itself as an imperfect realization of the idea which it is its essence to realize. To the question, what this imperfection is, Hegel's answer is as follows: 'bürgerliche Gesellschaft' is a society of consciously active subjects, whose activities are governed by law.[1] It is thus the realization or embodiment of a universal, since law is by its nature universal; and it is a genuine form of 'Sittlichkeit', because 'Sittlichkeit' is by definition the realization of the universal in acts of conscious will. The realization is, nevertheless, imperfect because although the activities of the individual in this sphere are directed by the universal, they are not directed upon it.[2] This is the 'sphere of particularity',[3] in which the proposed end of every action is individual satisfaction or private interest, and in which, therefore, though the law is fulfilled, its fulfilment is not conditioned by the conscious intention of fulfilling it. In the State, on the contrary, the universal is willed as an end; i.e. it is realized not merely in the sense that it receives embodiment, but in the further sense that it

[1] If law were not effective in governing their actions, they would not form a society at all, and there would be no sphere distinguishable at once from the State on the one hand and the State of Nature on the other.

[2] Hegel's expression that 'bürgerliche Gesellschaft' is 'die Erscheinungswelt des Sittlichen' (§ 181; cf. §§ 154, 189, 263, 266) has the implication that in this sphere the universal stands to the particulars in which it is realized, as *essence* ('Wesen') stands to the sensible appearance ('Erscheinung') in which it is embodied, or as form stands to matter in a natural object. It is the form by which, but not by the consciousness of which, the particulars are related to one another.

[3] §§ 181–5.

'CIVIL SOCIETY' AND STATE IN HEGEL 153

is made object of an understanding and purpose of a will.[1]

The difference between the economic and the ethical will is precisely that the former is governed in its exercise by law, the latter by consciousness of law; and this language of Hegel's seems naturally to bear the simple meaning that whereas 'bürgerliche Gesellschaft' is the sphere for the exercise of the economic will, 'Staat' is the sphere for the exercise of ethical will. It would follow from this that the two freedoms stand to one another in the same relation as the two spheres in which they are realized; and that, as 'bürgerliche Gesellschaft' is the imperfect realization of the idea realized perfectly in the State, so economic freedom, or freedom of choice, is the first and inadequate realization of the same freedom which is realized adequately only in the ethical will.

This is not merely a meaning which Hegel's words can bear; it is the meaning which, throughout a part of his work, they are intended to bear. The State is defined as the realization of 'Sittlichkeit',[2] and 'Sittlichkeit' as the actualization of what I have termed the ethical will.[3] This is the expression of that tendency in Hegel which I have called the Rationalist.

The difficulties of this doctrine begin as soon as we start to inquire more nearly into the meaning of the terms it uses. What is that 'universal' which is said to be realized without intention in 'bürgerliche Gesellschaft' and realized as an end of conscious will in the State? Is it the system of economic laws, by which the subjects' acts of particular self-interest are governed? If so, then we must take this doctrine to mean that the subject achieves ethical freedom

---

[1] § 266; cf. §§ 236, 249, 254. [2] See especially §§ 257–8.
[3] It is 'subjektive Gesinnung, aber des an sich seienden Rechts': § 141, and cf. §§ 142–50.

by making these laws the object of his consciousness,[1] and qualifies himself for membership of the State by a course of Political Economy; and this is clearly neither good sense nor what Hegel intends. Is it, then, the system of civil law, by which the economic activities of the subject are regulated and confined? But it is not true to say of this law that it operates unconsciously in the sphere of 'bürgerliche Gesellschaft', but in the State through the medium of a will conscious of it. This law is such that it cannot operate at all, except in so far as the subject is conscious of it and his will directed to its fulfilment. But will so directed is *ethical* will, and it follows therefore that, if civil law is realized in 'bürgerliche Gesellschaft', ethical will and therefore ethical freedom must be realized in it also.[2] But then where is the necessity for making the 'transition' from society to State?

The answer must be that there is no necessity. 'Bürgerliche Gesellschaft' itself contains all the conditions essential for the realization of 'Sittlichkeit', upon Hegel's own definition of that idea,[3] and when Hegel first introduces the State as the actualization of 'Sittlichkeit'[4] he endows it with no characteristic not already possessed by 'society' properly understood. Civil law is the system of law developed by logical necessity from the original principles of reason;[5] 'bürgerliche Gesellschaft' is the sphere in which this system

---

[1] Such consciousness would not, of course, really make his will 'ethical' nor his action free in the sense of being determined by the conception of a law. Since his acts are determined by the law equally whether he is conscious of it or not, his consciousness is not a necessary condition of this determination, but strictly epiphenomenal to it. Cf. Ch. I, p. 16 *sup*.

[2] We may sum up the difficulty thus: if the universal, of which Hegel speaks, is the universal of economic law, it can never be realized by an act of ethical will in the subject, but if it is the universal of civil law, it cannot be realized except by such an act.

[3] See §§ 142–50.   [4] §§ 257–8.

[5] This is the development of 'abstraktes Recht'. §§ 34–103.

'CIVIL SOCIETY' AND STATE IN HEGEL 155

is both 'posited'[1] and enforced.[2] It embodies, that is to say, a system of reasonable determinations and presents them as objective to the reason of the subject; and in doing this it fulfils all the conditions necessary to the perfect realization of ethical freedom.

When Hegel contrasts 'bürgerliche Gesellschaft' as the sphere of the economic will with 'Staat' as the realm of ethical freedom, he is not really contrasting 'society' with 'State' at all. He is contrasting the Empiricist[3] conception of society *with the Rationalist conception of society*. Thus he regards it as the characteristic defect of 'bürgerliche Gesellschaft', that although civil law is enforced in it, it is enforced solely to the end of the preservation of property and person,[4] i.e. as a means of securing economic satisfactions, and not as an end in itself. For this reason it presents itself to the subject who is compelled to obey it, as an external necessity[5] and an infringement of his liberty, not as a law which he recognizes as grounded in reason, and which he becomes free in obeying. But it is clear that this defect is not inherent in the nature of 'society', but springs only from a misapprehension of its nature. The remedy which it demands is not that the structure of society should be modified, or that it should 'pass over' into something else, but simply that the subject should submit himself to a moral education which will enable him to renounce the economic will, for which alone the law is a restriction, and to ascend to the standpoint at which he can recognize the system of law as the system of reason, in obedience to which his 'ethical' freedom consists.

(ii) That line of argument, it is clear, can never lead Hegel to the State at all. His doctrine of the State depends

[1] In which 'das Recht zum Gesetze wird'. See §§ 211-12, and especially § 217; cf. Ch. IV, p. 120 *sup*.   [2] §§ 219-28.
[3] The Lockian, e.g.   [4] §§ 157, 188, 208, 230.   [5] § 231.

upon an argument quite alien to Rationalism, and maintained by Hegel himself in constant polemic against it.[1] The difficulty of Hegel depends upon the fact that his own thought is never free from an element of Rationalism, and that he constantly uses the same language in an ambiguous sense to maintain at one time a Rationalist against an Empiricist position, at another to maintain a third position against either. Thus the language in which he expresses the relation of 'Staat' to 'bürgerliche Gesellschaft' may bear the sense which we have just ascribed to it, according to which it means no more than that 'society' on the Empiricist conception of it is an inadequate realization of what 'society' as conceived by Rationalism realizes adequately. But it may bear quite another meaning, and it is on this other meaning that Hegel relies when he makes the actual transition from 'bürgerliche Gesellschaft' to 'Staat'.

'Bürgerliche Gesellschaft' becomes 'Staat' when the law which is realized unconsciously in the former becomes the object of conscious will; and this will directed upon the universal is free in a sense in which the will directed upon a particular object and only directed *by* the universal is not. We have assumed hitherto that this fully free will is to be identified with the ethical will of the subject who submits himself to the law. But another identification is equally possible. It may be identified with the will which does not obey the law, but administers it, and the transition from 'bürgerliche Gesellschaft' to 'Staat' will then be the same in principle as the transition in Plato from the 'first city' to the ideal Polis. It is with the coming of a class of rulers that the operation of law ceases to be automatic and becomes the object of a conscious will, namely of the ruler's will.

'Absolute Sittlichkeit' is for Hegel the realization of law

[1] This is his polemic against the political philosophy of the 'Aufklärung' as represented by Kant.

'CIVIL SOCIETY' AND STATE IN HEGEL

in an act of will directed (not merely by it, but) upon it, and he does not ask himself whether this act is to be conceived as that of ruler or of subject. If the latter, 'bürgerliche Gesellschaft' supplies adequate conditions for its exercise: only when the ethical will is tacitly identified with the ruler's will does the State become necessary for its realization.

Hegel relies upon this tacit identification throughout his doctrine of the State. It is implied already in his account of those two institutions of Police[1] and Trade Guilds, or 'Corporations',[2] in which he sees a foretaste of 'absolute Sittlichkeit' within the sphere of 'bürgerliche Gesellschaft' itself, and which therefore serve to prepare the transition to the State. It is the business of Police to keep order,[3] and to punish breaches of order;[4] to exercise such general supervision and control over economic relationships as is exemplified in the inspection of wares exposed for sale in the open market,[5] and in the special provision for those members of society who are excluded by accident or ill health from participating in the common supply of wealth through the normal channel of an open labour market.[6] All these activities imply that the law has been made the object of understanding, and its realization willed. If order is enforced, the enforcing agent at least must know the order which he is enforcing; and interference with the economic relationships, say of consumer with producer, implies, as Hegel points out,[7] that the order by which their activities are governed has ceased to the extent of that interference to be (as the law, e.g., of supply and demand is) automatic and unwilled, and has become the object of a conscious purpose. But this knowing and willing of the universal is demanded

---

[1] 'Polizei.' §§ 231 ff. Hegel gives the term a wide meaning, including (see § 236 z) provision of public services and care of public health.
[2] 'Korporationen.' §§ 250 ff. They differ from Trade Unions in that they do not exclude the employer. [3] § 231.
[4] § 232. [5] § 236. [6] §§ 237-8. [7] § 236.

158 'CIVIL SOCIETY' AND STATE IN HEGEL

only in the man who exercises such control, not at all in the man who is subject to it.

Something the same is true of the trade-guild. An individual member of a purely economic society would be conscious only of his own particular end, but unconscious of the multifarious bonds by which his interest is connected with that of others and by which consequently his activity is determined in relation to that of others. In this respect he is exactly like the craftsman who is a member of Plato's 'first city', whose vision is so limited to the information of his own subject-matter that he cannot reflect it upon the form of which his own craft is subject-matter and by which its relation to other crafts is determined. In the 'Corporation' the bonds of common interest, which determine the action of individual members of a trade even when they are not recognized to be common, are made objects of conscious awareness and deliberate promotion. Thus, as Hegel says,[1] in the 'Corporation' the automatic regulation of particular activities by economic laws is replaced by a measure of conscious control; the universal or order is not merely realized, but is made the object of a will. But, once more, this will which wills the universal, and is therefore free, is the will which regulates, not which submits to regulation; a ruler's and not a subject's will.[2]

---
[1] § 249.

[2] This remains none the less true for the fact that the same individual doubles the parts of craftsman and guildsman. In so far as he is a craftsman, his gaze is fastened to the particular, his activities are determined by economic laws, and he enjoys only the freedom of the 'economic' will; *qua* guildsman he achieves the 'ethical' freedom of a will whose object is the law, but he achieves this freedom *not* in submitting to the law, but in administering, correcting, and controlling it.

It is important to add that in conceiving the two capacities of ruler and subject united in one individual, Hegel's doctrine of the guild marks a great advance over anything in Plato. It is as though Plato had made the craftsmen of his 'first city' capable of such a περιαγωγή τῆς ψυχῆς that they could liberate their understandings from confine-

'CIVIL SOCIETY' AND STATE IN HEGEL 159

There is one process in particular, of great importance to Hegel, which exemplifies the characteristic difference between 'bürgerliche Gesellschaft' and 'Staat'; namely that the universal or law which operates automatically in the former is made in the latter the object of conscious purpose. This is the process of the education or 'formation'[1] of the individual. Hegel is deeply impressed by the discipline exerted by 'society' upon the individual, and by the necessity which it imposes upon him of submitting to 'formation'.[2] This formation[3] is not the end which the member of such a society proposes to himself. The only end of which he is conscious is that of making a living. But as a necessary means to attaining that end he must adapt himself to the requirements of society and conform himself to certain universal standards. He must, first and foremost, acquire skill in the production of some commodity in general demand. This means that he must submit his faculties to a universal mould, and direct his actions no longer from personal motives, but by objective standards. So long as, and in so far as, he is engaged in the exercise of his craft, his operations are directed by no private whim, but are dictated to him by the necessities of his art and the requirements of his market, a standard which is universal and common to him with all his fellow craftsmen. And even

---

ment to the objects of their crafts to the apprehension of the form to which their crafts themselves were subject-matter. If Plato had done this, the introduction of a ruling class would have been superfluous (see Ch. I, p. 28 *sup.*).

Hegel, as I shall contend, does not succeed in extending to the political sphere the principle realized in the guilds: that the capacities of ruler and of subject should be united in the same individual.

[1] 'Bildung.'

[2] It is significant that in the 'Phänomenologie' (1807) the stage of society which corresponds most nearly to 'bürgerliche Gesellschaft' is called 'Das Reich der Bildung'.

[3] For the following see especially § 187.

beyond his craft he must, as an indispensable means to his personal success, renounce his private caprices and eccentricities, and conform himself to the social usages prevalent around him.

The State begins when this 'universal' to which the individual must conform is understood as an object and willed as an end, and when the process of his formation is deliberately directed. This conscious control is characteristic already of the institutions which anticipate the realization of 'absolute Sittlichkeit' within the sphere of 'bürgerliche Gesellschaft' itself. Both 'Police'[1] and Guild[2] are to provide for the training, social or technical, of those who are under their care. In the State, this provision is extended beyond the merely social or technical to include the whole education of a citizen; and the chief end of almost all *political* institutions is for Hegel that they should subserve the *information* of the subject.[3]

We have only to remark, once more, that this conscious control of education, characteristic of the State, though it necessitates an understanding of the end and a willing of the universal, necessitates it only in the educator, but not in the educated.

This will directed upon the universal, which is characteristic of the State, can be exercised only upon the material of other wills not so directed. I can keep order only if some people are liable to be disorderly, and I can educate only if some people are uneducated. Already in his account of 'bürgerliche Gesellschaft' Hegel has introduced a distinction of *class* between those whose will is directed upon the particular[4] and those, 'the universal class',[5] whose will is

---

[1] § 239.   [2] § 252.   [3] See further, pp. 168 ff., *inf*.
[4] 'Der Stand des Gewerbes', § 204.
[5] 'Der allgemeine Stand', § 202; cf. § 250. Hegel adds to these two classes another, the agricultural class (§ 202), which I omit to discuss. I should add that, although I have used the word 'class' throughout as

'CIVIL SOCIETY' AND STATE IN HEGEL

directed upon the universal, and who must, therefore, be exempted from the necessity of supplying their own economic wants.[1]

If this 'universal class' exercised only the ethical will by which the subject accepts the law, its discrimination would necessitate no transition from 'society' to State. But when Hegel proceeds, as he immediately does, to endow it, in virtue of this universal will, with the function of regulating the order of society,[2] he is ascribing to it an activity which can be exercised only in the State.

So soon as the 'will for the universal' ceases to mean the ethical will of the subject and is tacitly identified with the will of the ruler, the distinction between the class devoted to economic and the class devoted to ethical activity becomes the distinction between a subject and a governing class, and this is the essence of the transition from 'society' to the State.

The 'will for the universal', though it is still called by the same name of the 'ethical will', is now a will which can be exercised by no citizen in a private station, but only by a public servant acting in his public capacity.[3] This govern-

the nearest equivalent of the German 'Stand', I doubt whether it is an exact equivalent. 'Class' seems to contain a stronger implication of hereditary membership than the German word contains, and I must ask the reader, therefore, to discount this implication throughout.

[1] § 205.

[2] §§ 205, 303. Hegel, of course, does not *recognize* that in attributing to the 'universal class' a regulative function he is doing more than attributing to it simply an 'ethical will', in the sense in which the subject in society may be said to possess one. This is an instance of a confusion which runs through Hegel's political philosophy on this point. He does not see that the Rationalist opposition between particular and universal will is not the same as the Platonic; that the former is the opposition between economic and ethical will in the subject, the latter between the subject's will and the ruler's.

[3] See the important § 157, especially the significant words '... die Wirklichkeit des substantiellen Allgemeinen, und des demselben gewidmeten *öffentlichen Lebens*' (my italics). Cf. § 303: 'Der allgemeine,

ing class *is* the State, and only those who are members of it can be said properly to 'have a life in the State' at all. The doctrine of the State, in consequence, in so far as it is distinct from the doctrine of society, is concerned almost[1] exclusively with the organization of this class and with the distribution of the governmental powers.[2]

The conclusion of all this is as follows: if the ethical will is identified with the will of the ruler, then it will be true that the State is the necessary condition of its exercise, but it will be true also that its exercise is confined to a limited body of men. In their will alone 'absolute Sittlichkeit' will be realized, and they alone will possess full ethical freedom;[3] and the possession of this freedom and the realization of this Sittlichkeit will presuppose the existence of another body of men excluded from participation in either.

But if this identification is not made, then, as we have seen, Hegel has no ground for making the transition from 'society' to State at all.

It is almost superfluous to emphasize the Platonism of Hegel's transition from 'society' to State; it is identical in principle with Plato's transition from the 'first city' to the

näher dem Dienst der Regierung sich widmende Stand.' In § 310 the 'Sinn des Staates' is treated as synonymous with 'der obrigkeitliche Sinn'. Cf. § 302, 'Der Sinn und die Gesinnung des Staats und der Regierung'. [1] Not quite; see p. 168 *inf.*

[2] See § 269. 'Diese unterschiedenen Seiten [sc. des Organismus des Staates] sind ... die verschiedenen *Gewalten* und deren Geschäfte und Wirksamkeiten ...; dieser Organismus ist die politische Verfassung' (my italics). It is implied that the 'organism of the state' is identical with the organization of government.

In precisely the same way, Plato's doctrine of the Polis, as distinct from his account of the 'first city', is concerned exclusively with the organization of the rulers. (His neglect of the subject class is so complete that it has been possible even to raise doubts whether it is to be conceived as communistically organized or not!)

[3] In one of Hegel's earlier political works, the prototype of this ruling class is called 'der Stand der Freien'. *Wissenchaftliche Behandlungsarten des Naturrechts*, Werke, ed. Lasson, vol. vii, 2nd ed., p. 375.

'CIVIL SOCIETY' AND STATE IN HEGEL 163

ideal Polis. The 'universal class' corresponds to Plato's guardians.[1] The inclusion of this class within society transforms it at once from a civil and economic to a political society. Since the activity of governing is thus the distinguishing feature of political society, the operations of government and the organization of the governing power become for Hegel, as for Plato, the primary object of political, as opposed to social, philosophy.[2] The social organization, finally, upon which the government is conceived to have supervened persists, both for Hegel and for Plato, within the political society itself as the order characteristic of a subject class,[3] which is necessary to the

[1] The essential characteristic of this class is that it makes the universal the end of its activity (§ 303), and since both the knowledge and the willing of the universal are for Hegel the actualization of the faculty of thought ('Der Wille ist . . . das Denken . . . als Trieb sich Dasein zu geben' § 4 z; cf. the words in § 308 A, '. . . als denkendes . . . Bewußtsein und Wollen des Allgemeinen zu sein'), it must share with Plato's Rulers the virtue of Sophia; it must share with his Auxiliaries the virtue of Andreia inasmuch as 'der Militärstand ist der Stand der Allgemeinheit' (§ 327 z). I have been concerned to lay stress exclusively upon the essential point, that the Hegelian is identical with the Platonic political philosophy in its separation of a ruling from a subject class. But it must be noticed that Hegel's theory of government represents an advance over Plato's in some important respects, all tending towards the end of bridging the gulf which Plato had fixed between ruler and ruled. Thus (1) Hegel's governing class is a bureaucracy rather than an aristocracy; entry into it is not by birth only, but is *ouverte aux talents*, and is thus not closed to those born into the subject class (see § 291). (2) Hegel insists upon the importance of the specialization of the functions of government, as being essential to the *organic* unity of the whole. This specialization had been absent from the organization of Plato's ruling class (except for the single subdivision of the guardians into rulers and fighters), and its introduction is significant because it extends to the ruling community the principle of division of labour which was necessarily confined for Plato to the economic order of the subject class (see § 290).

[2] See p. 162, n. 2, *sup*.

[3] Hegel refers to them in § 314 as 'those members of the "bürgerliche Gesellschaft" who have no share in the government'.

activity of the governing will as the subject-matter upon which it is exercised.

The discrimination of rulers and subjects into classes is a relic of Platonism in Hegel's philosophy of the State; his doctrine that the State is the product of a timeless process, of which the stages stand to one another in a relation of logical consequence, is a relic of Platonism in his metaphysics. There seems to be a necessary connexion between this metaphysical and that political doctrine.

If we ask: What, on Hegel's doctrine, is actually the relation between 'bürgerliche Gesellschaft' and State? the answer must be twofold. (i) They are stages in the timeless process of dialectic; and that is to say, they do not stand to one another in any real relation, either spatial or temporal, at all, but, as products of a metaphysical division, can be distinguished only as *logically* prior or consequent to one another. This doctrine is itself Platonic, if we were right in saying[1] that Plato's account of the passage from 'first city' to ideal Polis as a process in time was only a myth, representing as successive stages the matter and form of the Polis which are only logically distinguishable.

But (ii) the conception that men are related to law as matter to form, which excludes the possibility that there might have been a state *historically* prior to the imposition of law (because matter cannot exist without form), and which, therefore, necessitates this conclusion that the prepolitical states of society are related to the State itself only as logical antecedents—this conception is itself the very ground of the distinction of classes within the State itself. *Because* men are related to law as matter to form, *therefore* the work of imposing (or reimposing) form must be the task of a ruler related to his subjects as craftsman to subject-

[1] p. 142 *sup.*

'CIVIL SOCIETY' AND STATE IN HEGEL

matter. Hegel and Plato are alike compelled to conceive each term of their *metaphysical* division to be embodied as a separate class within the actual State.[1] These *classes* are not related ideally to one another, nor are they the product of a merely metaphysical division; they are, on the contrary, coeval in time, juxtaposed in space, and bound by the real relation of ruling and subjection.

I should be going at once beyond my subject and beyond my depth if I tried to push this inquiry much further, but it is relevant to recur for a moment to what was said about Hobbes at the beginning of this chapter.[2] It is characteristic of Hobbes that he does attribute something more than a merely logical priority to the pre-social state of man, and that his account of the development of the State claims to be something other than a metaphysical analysis clothed in myth. The ascription of real temporal priority to the State of Nature is equivalent to a denial of the assumption that man, outside the State, is nothing but matter awaiting form, and, therefore, equally of the implication that his relation to the ruler within the State is that of subject-matter to craftsman. The insistence that the State is to be understood as the product not of a logical but of an historical development, of which the stages are past-historical epochs,[3] seems to remove the necessity of conceiving inequality among its citizens as essential to the State. There will still be inequality, but not inequality of contemporaries, or *class* inequality. The inequality will lie between the citizen of the State and his less civilized predecessor, not between the citizen of the State and his unenfranchized neighbour.

[1] Hegel uses the term 'bürgerliche Gesellschaft' to refer not only to an ideal stage in the development of the State, but to an actual class of persons within it. Cf. p. 163, n. 3, *sup*.   [2] p. 144 *sup*.
[3] I do not, of course, mean that Hobbes was correct in his description of the condition which he asserted to be historically antecedent to the formation of the State.

Contrasted with the doctrine implicit in Hobbes, that the State is to be understood as the product of a temporal series of states, the Hegelian doctrine that it is to be understood only as the product of a logical development appears, and is, uncompromisingly Platonic. But the advance of the Hegelian over the Platonic metaphysic is an advance towards the lessening of this contrast. Hegel's 'idea' differs from Plato's in being 'dialectical', that is to say, in containing within itself the efficient cause of its own development. This development *is not* an historical development, because it is held to be timeless; but it is nearer to it than the Platonic 'idea' to which all process was extrinsic.

I am not, of course, holding up Hobbes as an ideal towards which Hegel only faintly approximates. He does seize upon one important element, that of temporal sequence, which is lacking from the Hegelian dialectic, but he seizes upon it to the exclusion of everything else. Temporal sequence *is not* historical development, although historical development is not without temporal sequence. Hobbes conceives succession in time without development, as Hegel conceives development without time.

The source from which this most un-Greek idea of explaining a thing by its temporal history was introduced into European philosophy is, of course, the same as that from which have been derived almost all the un-Greek elements of European philosophy, that is to say, almost everything in European philosophy which is, by contrast with the Greek, specifically modern: namely the Christian revelation. The service of the Empiricist philosophy has been the same here as elsewhere: stubbornly to maintain the truths (or some of the truths) of Christian dogma against the danger of too hasty rationalization. Here, as elsewhere, it is the distinctive characteristic of the Hegelian philosophy that it has advanced beyond the Greek standpoint by the

'CIVIL SOCIETY' AND STATE IN HEGEL

assimilation of Christian elements, but that it fails in not being Christianized enough.

We must return from this digression to the point which the argument had reached on page 164.

What, it may well be asked, has become of the doctrine, maintained by Hegel himself in constant polemic against Plato, according to which the realization of Sittlichkeit in the State was based, as its realization in the Polis was not, upon the freedom of the subject? Has this doctrine disappeared without a trace when the level of the State is reached? Do the 'subjective freedoms' remain confined to the ideal stage of 'bürgerliche Gesellschaft'? Are they actualized in no real rights exercised by the subject within the State itself and reflected in no institutions within the political constitution?

These questions are not completely answered by pointing out, what is no doubt true, that as the organization of 'bürgerliche Gesellschaft' is retained as the organization of a class within the State itself,[1] the members of this class must still enjoy the freedom, both ethical and economic, of which this order is the condition. This order can be maintained in a class within the State only in so far as it is respected by the government as constituting a limitation of its authority. The members of this class, therefore, do not enjoy this freedom in the capacity of political subjects. They are not free in their subjection to the ruler's will, but precisely in so far as they are exempt from such subjection. What we are asking is whether the freedom which the subject possesses as member of 'bürgerliche Gesellschaft' extends also to the actions which he performs in the capacity of political subject in obedience to the commands of a governor, not in a sphere exempt from governmental control.

[1] p. 163 *sup.*

168 'CIVIL SOCIETY' AND STATE IN HEGEL

The answer must be that the doctrine of 'subjective freedom' is not without a further modifying influence upon Hegel's theory of the State itself. The whole of that theory is not exhausted in the account we have so far given of it. Hegel's attention is not directed exclusively, as Plato's is, upon the organization of the ruling class, nor is his theory of the political constitution confined entirely to the institutions of government. He explicitly distinguishes two elements in the constitution from the governmental power: the monarchical[1] and the 'parliamentary' element.[2] It is the latter which we have now to consider. Hegel comprises under this designation those democratic institutions which are organs of politics and not of government, and to which there is no counterpart whatever in the political philosophy of Plato: the institutions, namely, of Free Speech, Free Press, organized Public Opinion, Parliament, Party, and Representation. These institutions are for Hegel the conditions within the political sphere of the freedom of the subject class,[3] and their whole *raison d'être* is that they secure a realization within the political sphere for those freedoms of the subject which are characteristic of the sphere of 'bürgerliche Gesellschaft'.[4] The distinction between the two freedoms realized in the subject of 'society' has its counterpart in an analogous distinction within the political freedom secured by parliamentary institutions. The subject of the State enjoys one freedom analogous to, but not identical with, the ethical freedom, and another freedom analogous to, but not identical with, the economic freedom of the member of 'society'. It will be convenient to consider these

---

[1] §§ 275-86.   [2] 'Das ständische Element.' §§ 301-20.
[3] Or, as he expresses it (§ 314), of 'those members of "civil society" who have no share in the government'. Cf. § 303, 'In dem ständischen Elemente der gesetzgebenden Gewalt kommt der Privatstand [contrast 'der allgemeine Stand'] zu einer politischen Bedeutung und Wirksamkeit'.
[4] See § 301 A, *ad fin.*

'CIVIL SOCIETY' AND STATE IN HEGEL

freedoms of the political subject separately, and first that one which is analogous to the ethical freedom of 'society'; but it must be remembered that Hegel himself recognizes no distinction either between the 'social' and the 'political' freedom of the subject, or between the two species into which each is subdivided.[1]

(i) Parliamentary institutions secure the condition of a freedom analogous to ethical freedom in the subject of the State in so far as they are the media by which he is not merely informed about the steps taken and decisions made by the government, but enlightened by an understanding of the grounds which make them necessary.[2] So understood, they lose the character of arbitrary commands; the subject can accept them as reasonable and so embrace them as something not foreign to himself. The sentiment which supervenes upon understanding[3] and makes acceptance spontaneous is what Hegel calls 'politische Gesinnung' or patriotism.[4] It is thus the condition both of the realization of the governmental enactments[5] and of the subject's freedom in submitting to them.[6]

Obviously this doctrine is closely similar to that which established that ethical freedom in the subject, of which

---

[1] I shall henceforth distinguish as the 'patriotic' and the 'political' wills those subjective activities of the political subject which are analogous respectively to the ethical and economic wills in the member of 'bürgerliche Gesellschaft'.

[2] Cf. § 314, § 315 and § 315 z, § 317. To secure this end debates in Parliament must be public.

[3] I should perhaps remark that Hegel does not think it necessary for the third, or agricultural, class in the State (see p. 160, n. 5, *sup.*), which I am omitting from consideration, that the patriotic sentiment should be based on conscious insight. With them it is based upon *trust*. But insight is a necessary condition of its restoration in the class ('der Stand des Gewerbes') which comes into existence only when its members are emancipated from such naïve dependence.

[4] § 268.   [5] § 289.   [6] § 268.

'bürgerliche Gesellschaft' could supply the conditions, and Hegel nowhere shows any recognition that it is not identical with it.[1] We have to inquire how far this identification is justified, and how far it rests upon a confusion.

The object of ethical will is both reasonable and universal. A system of law can claim acceptance by such a will in so far as it can be derived by speculative reason from logical principles; or, as Hegel says, in so far as it follows 'out of the concept'. The local and temporal accidents of its particular embodiment as this or that historical State are no proper object of reason, but of a merely historical knowledge.[2] Not these, therefore, but the universal determinations of 'the State' as such are objects in willing which the subject is free.

By drawing a distinction between essential and accidental within the State itself,[3] and by claiming to exhibit the former as a necessary development of the dialectic, Hegel has been enabled to extend to the essentials of the constitution, that is to say, to those institutions without which a State would not be a State, the same authority for the ethical will of the subject, and one based upon the same possibility of reasonable deduction, which his Rationalist predecessors had confined to the Law of Nature, or to the civil law of 'society'. On this ground and to this extent he can maintain that the possibility of ethical freedom is preserved for the subject of the State.

But the understanding which is the condition of this freedom is one which parliamentary institutions are quite

---

[1] In 317 z, e.g., freedom of speech is justified by language precisely similar to that which was employed of the ethical freedom proper to the subject of 'bürgerliche Gesellschaft'. It begins: 'Das Prinzip der modernen Welt fordert, daß, was jeder anerkennen soll, sich ihm als ein Berechtigtes zeige.' Again, publicity of parliamentary proceedings is demanded on no other ground than that adduced for publicity of proceedings in the courts for the enforcement of civil law (cf. § 14 with § 224).

[2] Ch. IV, p. 117–18 *sup.*   [3] Ch. IV, p. 133 *sup.*

patently not adapted to supply. Insight into the reasonable necessity of the essentials of the constitution is obviously to be acquired, if Hegel is to remain consistent with himself, not by perusal of journals and debates, but by painful study of the *Philosophie des Rechts*. Nor is the ethical sentiment which is conditioned by such philosophical understanding to be identified with the sentiment of patriotism. The one is evoked by the universal, but the other by the individual; the latter feeds upon that very historical peculiarity which is indifferent to the former.

Patriotism begins only where, upon Hegel's doctrine, the possibility of derivation 'from the concept' ceases and where law becomes *positive* in the proper sense of the word. It is displayed in the acceptance of particular regulations which are susceptible not of a philosophical but solely of an historical explanation. These are necessary and not arbitrary; but they are necessary not in the sense that they are involved in the concept of the State as such, but in the sense that they are demanded by the temporal interest of this particular State now. This necessitation, which appears to the forward look of the statesman as national expediency and makes the temporal course of events intelligible to the backward look of the political historian, is the only necessitation upon which the subject can derive enlightenment from the publicity of parliamentary institutions.

Granted that an historical reason may be discerned in those particulars of policy which lie below the possibility of universal determination; that this reason is made accessible by parliamentary institutions to the understanding of the political subject; that this understanding evokes in him a sentiment of patriotism in virtue of which he so identifies himself with the interest of his country that he wills freely what the situation demands: it is still only by a confusion that the patriotic can be identified with the ethical will which is the response to a perception of a wholly different kind of reason.[1]

It is only by such a confusion that Hegel can maintain at the same time the two following positions: *both* that the State can be philosophically derived by a process of necessary reasoning, *and* that the subject of an historical State can have access to no supra-temporal standard by which he can stand in judgement over it. The conjunction of these two positions may almost be called the kernel of the whole Hegelian philosophy of the state. Each taken by itself is Platonic; but Hegel has already surrendered the Platonic presupposition which alone can render them consistent with one another. If the State is susceptible of metaphysical grounding and can be understood by the philosophical reason to be implied in the eternal nature of things, then this metaphysical ground is at once the justification of the authority which an actual State claims over its subjects and the standard by which the imperfections of any particular State can be judged. But then there is only one ground upon which access to this standard of judgement can be denied to the subject himself: namely that he is incapable of the exercise of philosophical reason, and is, therefore, inferior to those who are capable of it. Plato accepts this ground, but Hegel is bound to deny it in order to maintain the ethical freedom of the subject. He can then avoid the conclusion of his Rationalist predecessors,[2] that every subject has access

---

[1] This confusion may be illustrated from the following passage (§ 315): 'Die Eröffnung dieser Gelegenheit von Kenntnissen hat die allgemeinere Seite, daß so die öffentliche Meinung erst zu wahrhaften Gedanken und zur Einsicht in den *Zustand und Begriff* des Staates und dessen Angelegenheiten, und damit erst zu einer Fähigkeit, darüber vernünftiger zu urteilen, kommt' (my italics). Publicity of parliamentary proceedings can certainly enlighten the subject about the historical situation ('Zustand'), but hardly about the logical concept ('Begriff') of the State.

[2] The philosophers of 'Aufklärung'.

to a supra-temporal standard by which he can judge the State to which he belongs, only by the apparent subterfuge of debasing the insight ascribed to the subject from that philosophical understanding, which implies a reference to a supra-temporal ground, to that historical understanding, which does not.

Most of the traditional criticism of Hegel has accepted the former of these two positions and repudiated the latter from that standpoint. That the subject should recognize the binding authority of the eternal reason disclosed by philosophical speculation as the ground of nature has seemed no derogation to his dignity as a man. But that he should attribute a similar authority to a temporal power which has come to be in an historical process, appeared nothing less than an abdication of his moral autonomy. To accept this criticism is, of course, to revert to that Rationalism for which the State (as distinct from 'civil society') is not intelligible at all.

In reality, however, of these two incompatible positions, it is the latter which contains the germ of a new truth, while the former is only the empty shell of an old one. The way out of the contradiction is by discarding the former, not by repudiating the latter. To be limited to an historical understanding of the State is a debasement only if it implies exclusion from some higher understanding, such as that philosophical understanding, possession of which constituted the superiority of Plato's rulers. Hegel retains a belief in this superior or philosophical understanding of the State; but he does not, as in consistency he should, attribute it to his class of rulers as their title to superiority. The *Philosophie des Rechts* is no more the handbook of the statesman than it is the intelligencer of the subject, for the ruler has to guide his policy by the temporal necessities of an historical situation.

'CIVIL SOCIETY' AND STATE IN HEGEL

It appears upon examination that the superior, philosophical understanding of the State, by comparison with which historical knowledge is degraded, is possessed *only* by the professional philosopher. Neither the ruler needs it to direct his policy, nor the subject to secure his freedom. That it should be so very useless awakens the first suspicions of its superiority. Surely an understanding of the very nature of the State would be a condition of the ruler's ruling well and of the subject's obeying freely? And hard upon the heels of that suspicion will follow the conviction that the whole dialectical or metaphysical deduction of the State must miss its true nature, and that the real business of the philosopher is that historical understanding which makes the ruler a statesman and the subject free.[1]

---

[1] I will add here two remarks which may serve to avert misunderstanding. (i) If a logical deduction of the essence of the State is possible, then historical understanding is necessarily confined to its accidents. It is hard to realize that historical understanding is freed from this confinement when the logical deduction is found to be impossible. We acquiesce too readily in the conclusion that historical understanding, though admitted to be the only understanding of which we are capable, is still an understanding only of the accidental; and thus the ghost of logic still scares us from setting foot in the domain which logic once ruled. The historical understanding is freed from this confinement only when it proceeds itself to the occupation of this derelict domain. Thus if we reject the 'speculative' deduction of the State and retain only the historical understanding of it, we are not thereby committed to the conclusion that this understanding is confined to those elements in the State which Hegel excluded from his speculative deduction. The stages of this deduction, 'abstraktes Recht', 'Moralität', and the rest are not to be simply discarded either as irrelevant to the understanding of the State or as inaccessible to human reason, but they are to be understood for what they really are, namely for historical realities ('abstraktes Recht', say the system of Roman Law, 'Moralität', say Lutheran Pietism), and all that is to be discarded is the sham of a logical necessitation. But when this is done, historical understanding has been extended to the essentials of the State.

(This may be illustrated from the sphere of biology. The historical understanding in this science underwent a similar extension in the moment when biology became evolutionary. So long as the specific

(ii) But parliamentary institutions have another function for Hegel besides that enlightenment of the historical understanding which evokes the patriotic will.

essence was conceived to be timeless, it was held to be the object of a non-historical understanding, and natural *history* was confined to the inessential. The discovery that species were not immutable did not condemn the science of biology to a perpetual self-limitation to the historical knowledge of the inessential; instead, the recognition that species themselves were the products of a temporal development, extended historical understanding to the very sphere which had been previously reserved to a non-historical understanding.)

We may consider the matter similarly from the point of view of the subject of the State. If the right of the State is deducible from some timeless standard, such as the Moral Law, then his historical understanding is confined to the sources not of the State's right but only of its power, and to claim his obedience upon the ground of such understanding is an affront to his dignity as a moral being. But if the conception of the Moral Law itself is discovered to be the product of an historical development (to have been the fruit, let us say, of the assimilation of the system of Roman Law into the tradition of Christian ethics), then the historical understanding will extend to the source of the State's right no less than to that of its power.

So long as these elements which States have in common ('abstraktes Recht', 'Moralität', e.g.) are held, as they are by Hegel, to be of timeless derivation, and historical understanding is thus confined to what differentiates individual States from one another, the patriotism which is based upon the latter must be narrowly and exclusively national, and it must conflict, or be capable of conflicting, with the ethical sentiment based upon the non-historical apprehension of the universal right (*jus gentium*). When this conflict occurs, the patriotic sentiment is immoral, and prejudice arises against Hegel for maintaining that in cases of such conflict patriotism must and should prevail over ethical sentiment. The opponents of whom I am thinking maintain against Hegel the opposite thesis: that ethical should prevail over patriotic sentiment. Of these opposing theses it must be said that neither is right, but that Hegel's represents the dawning of a truth which has never appeared above the horizon of his opponent's vision: the truth that the only true understanding is historical understanding and that the only true allegiance is allegiance based on it. Hegel's failure consists, not in his recognition of the superiority of the historical understanding, but in his restriction of its sphere. He implies the nullity of the non-historical reason, and yet he respects the integrity of its domain. An historical understanding excluded from the universal principles of 'Recht' and 'Moralität' *is* narrow, and a patriotism based upon it must be wrong. But

'CIVIL SOCIETY' AND STATE IN HEGEL

Just as in 'bürgerliche Gesellschaft' the system of civil law had the double function of providing at once a universal object upon which ethical will might be directed, and a system of private property within which particular desires might find unhindered satisfaction; parliamentary institutions in the State have not only the function of informing the opinion of the individual, but also the quite different function of providing an expression for his uninformed opinion. They have not only to make his will general, by conforming it to a universal mould; they have to give free play also to the utterance of his particular will. Thus the freedom of public opinion, whose organs are the institutions of free speech and a free press, consists in 'the satisfaction of that restless craving, to utter one's opinion and to have said one's say'.[1] Public opinion provides the expression of that 'formal, subjective freedom' which the individual enjoys when he can 'form and utter simply as an individual his own judgement, his own opinion, and his own advice about matters of general concern'.[2] Such utterance of

the remedy of its narrowness is to extend it. When 'Right' and 'Morality' are themselves understood to be the products of an historical development, then the historical understanding is released from its confinement to what is particular to an individual State, and the allegiance based upon it has been widened beyond national patriotism to embrace at least the whole of Christendom and of the civilization sprung from it.

(ii) Historical understanding does not exclude criticism, but only criticism by reference to a standard conceivable as end or essence and as such definable apart from the object in which it is embodied. It excludes, in other words, such criticism as we apply to the products of the useful arts, when we judge them by reference to a distinct conception of their end or purpose; but it does not exclude such criticism as we apply to works of fine art. In this sphere it has long been recognized as the vice of criticism to endeavour to apply a standard conceivable apart from the work criticized, as end is conceivable apart from performance; but criticism has remained possible without such an application. The reformation required in philosophy is only that which has already taken place in biology and in the criticism of art.

[1] § 319.   [2] § 316.

'CIVIL SOCIETY' AND STATE IN HEGEL 177

opinion, whether in public or in parliament, is not valuable for its effect upon public decisions.[1] On the contrary, its sole justification is that it remains without effect. Hegel compares it to the licence of mocking their general enjoyed during the triumphal procession by the Roman soldiery, who thus 'wreaked upon him a harmless revenge for their hard service and subordination, and set themselves on a temporary equality with him'.[2] The value of the institutions, by which a similar licence is afforded to the subject of the State, is thus precisely that of a safety-valve;[3] they give a vent in speech to the private ambitions which the law suppresses in the subject, and which, if allowed no such vent, could work themselves out only in lawless actions.

Hegel designates this licence by his customary term as 'subjective freedom',[4] and he applies to it his customary remark that it is demanded by the 'principle of the modern world'.[5] It is, nevertheless, different from any of those kinds of freedom which we have hitherto distinguished. This 'political' will differs from the 'patriotic' will in a manner analogous to that in which the economic differs from the ethical will, in that it is determined by no precedent act of understanding, but is an immediate ebullition of particular desire. But it is not the economic will. It neither displays any regularity in its operation corresponding to that of economic laws, nor, above all, does it issue, as the economic will does,[6] in the fulfilment of the law by which it is controlled.

There are thus not less than five different practical activities which Hegel includes in his State under the title of 'subjective freedom': the ruler's will, and four different wills proper to the subject, the ethical, the economic, the 'patriotic' and the 'political'. If *all* these activities are to be

---
[1] § 314.   [2] § 319 A, freely translated.   [3] See § 317 z.
[4] § 316.   [5] § 317.   [6] Ch. IV, p. 130 *sup*.

called 'sittlich', then 'sittlich' simply means any practical activity which can be admitted within the State and gives no definition whatever of the character in virtue of which it is admissible. If 'sittlich' is defined in the strictest sense which it can bear, and is applied to those activities which are determined by the concept of a universal law to the fulfilment of it, then it can be applied only to the ethical will of those distinguished above, and possibly to the ruler's will, in so far as it is held to be determined by other grounds than those of political necessity; if the definition is so loosened that historical understanding may take the place of the concept of a universal law, the denotation of the term may be extended to include both the 'patriotic' will and the remaining activities of the ruler; if it is still further loosened, so as to apply to all activities, however determined, which result in the fulfilment of law, it will include the activities of the economic will. But I do not see how it can be extended to cover the 'political' will and remain a definition at all.

The political will is without an antitype in Plato's Polis. The ruler's will in Hegel is foreshadowed in Plato's ruler's will, the ethical will in the will of the auxiliaries. Even the economic will may be found, if we follow not so much what Plato says as the implications of what he says, to be presupposed as the spring of the economic activities of the Third Class and to be justified on the condition that it is ordered by law. But the political will is not amenable to such order. It is by its nature contrary to justice, and it can manifest itself only in Stasis, which is by definition the destruction of the unity which constitutes at once the essence and the 'virtue' of the Polis.

Hegel admits this will into his State with a manifest reluctance. An asperity creeps into his language when he speaks of it, and there is something almost laughable to an

English mind in the nervous solicitude of the precautions with which he seeks to ensure that, although it is not debarred from expression in speech, it shall be entirely without practical effect. Nevertheless, the fact that he admits it is of great significance, because to admit it is to attribute a worth to it, and thus involves the recognition of a worth in will other than its conformity to reason.

VI

RULER AND SOVEREIGN

THE highest form of activity which the Greeks could conceive was the theoretical; the highest form of practical activity which they could conceive was that exemplified by a Techne and exercised by a Demiurge. The essential characteristics of the activity of the Demiurge are (i) that it is purposive, (ii) that it is informative.

(i) The operation of the Demiurge is determined by a form which is at once the end of his activity and the essence of his product. This form must be conceived antecedently to the operation by an act of theoretical reason, and the productive activity of the craftsman must be determined wholly by the form conceived as end. It is easy to see why such an act represented for the Greeks the highest form of practical activity; it was the act in which will was wholly subordinated to, and determined by, the theoretical reason.

(ii) The operation of the Demiurge is confined to the information of a given matter. This limitation follows directly from the former, since if the operation is to be governed by reason, it must be confined to the realization of the intelligible, and form only, not matter, is intelligible.

The highest form of activity is that which must be attributed to God, and hence the essential activity of the god of Greek philosophy is the theoretical activity of reason. To deny that the practical activity is divine is to deny that God acts by efficient causation upon the world. His activity is directed solely upon himself, and he can move the world only as unmoved mover, or final cause.

But Greek philosophy was not unanimously content with

this conclusion. God was endowed also[1] with a practical activity, and conceived as efficient cause of the world. What it concerns us to observe is that the activity then attributed to God is precisely that which, as we have seen above, the Greeks were bound to conceive as the highest practical activity; the activity of a Demiurge. His activity is that of realizing the forms by embodying them in matter, but neither the forms, nor the matter in which they are embodied, are the product of his activity.

The Christian doctrine of God as *Creator* implies a quite different conception of the divine activity from any which the Greeks achieved. It is not merely different in ascribing to God a practical activity and a relation of efficient causality to the world. The conception of God as Demiurge had done so much. But it is different in the nature of the practical activity which is attributed to God.

Creative activity is free not from one only, but from both of the limitations to which the activity of the Demiurge is subject. It is neither limited by a given matter, nor determined by a given form. Its freedom from the former of these limitations has been recognized widely enough; that only is created of which the matter itself is produced *ex nihilo*. It is its freedom from the latter which more particularly concerns us here. If the form has no being distinct from its realization, it is impossible that the creative act should be determined by the antecedent conception of it as an end, and hence impossible also that this practical activity should be determined by a prior theoretical one. In other words, the doctrine of Creation contains the implication that the divine, and therefore the highest, form of practical activity is not determined by reason.

The same implication is contained in the closely connected conception of God as Commander. The divine law

[1] As by Plato in the *Timaeus*.

is a categorical imperative, directed to the achievement of no end, and therefore the practical activity from which it issues is determined by no precedent theoretical conception.

This Christian doctrine of the divine activity is the source from which the distinguishing characteristics of modern political theory[1] have been derived. It is the source, in particular, of the conception of the sovereign, which gradually displaced the Greek conception of the ruler as the supreme authority in political society.

The activity of the ruler is for Plato the only activity in which man realizes all his virtue, and, as the highest human activity, it partakes of the nature of the activity of God. As God, so the ruler achieves the highest perfection of his nature in a purely theoretical activity; and when he abandons this highest level and descends to the work of ruling, the practical activity in which he then engages is, like that of God, the activity of a Demiurge.

The activity of ruling, that is to say, is both purposive and informative. From each of these two characteristics one of the main features of the Platonic political theory follows as a necessary consequence.

(1) It is purposive, that is to say it is directed by a form conceived as end, not itself product of the activity which it informs and hence discernible as essence from historical accident within the state produced by this activity. Such discrimination of formal from material within the actual is the presupposition of the possibility of a philosophy of the Polis, according to the Greek conception of philosophy; that is to say a science of which the organ is reason freed from dependence upon sense,[2] and of which the object is

[1] And indeed of modern political practice.
[2] This means simply that the Greeks held philosophy to be a demonstrative science, i.e. one of which the conclusions did not depend upon

RULER AND SOVEREIGN

the essential in distinction from the accidental, the universal in distinction from the particular, the intelligible in distinction from the sensible. A state which was the work of a Demiurge would be the proper object of a metaphysical theory, because in it this discrimination of formal from material elements would be possible.

(2) It is informative only. This concept of information runs through Plato's political theory from top to bottom. The essential activity of man *qua* artist is to inform his material, of man *qua* political subject to submit himself as material to a similar process of information, of man *qua* ruler to inform the subject. The activity neither of the ruler nor of the artificer brings anything into being; each weds a form, which is eternal, to a matter, which is given.

I wish to show that the characteristic developments of modern political theory have depended upon the displacement of the concept of information by that of creation as the highest practical activity, but I will preface the attempt by a digression intended to show how the same displacement has influenced the modern conception of artistic activity.

Art appeared to Plato to have value precisely in so far as it was not creative. The artist's activity was governed by reason only in so far as it was limited to the execution of an idea previously conceived by the intellect. It produced the idea no more than it produced the material, but was confined to the embodiment of the preconceived form as it was

empirical *evidence*. How far even a demonstrative science (such as Euclidean geometry, e.g.) may be dependent upon experience of sensible objects, either as means to the attainment of the concepts employed in reasoning or as illustrations continuously accompanying the process of reasoning itself, is a different question by which the former is not affected. The question at issue between Plato and Aristotle is solely that of the dependence of reason upon experience in the latter sense; neither questioned the assumption that the conclusions of reason must be free from dependence upon empirical evidence.

confined to the information of the pre-existent matter. An inability in the artist to render an account of the idea which his work embodied was not for Plato a sign that his activity was more than a Techne, but a sign that it was less. It did not mean that he was doing anything else than carrying out an idea in the information of a given matter, but only that he was carrying it out without knowing what he was doing. He is in the position of the metal-worker who should turn out a pair of compasses, without any knowledge of the nature of a circle. His success in producing such an object would not entitle him to be regarded as a better craftsman than he who designs compasses for the express purpose of drawing circles; indeed it is not to be ascribed to his skill, but to chance, or divine intervention. This failure to conceive beforehand, and inability to render an account afterwards, is characteristic of most of the forms of what we should regard as the highest art, of poetry for example. Such forms of art remain therefore a complete mystery for Plato. He has either to maintain that these artists achieve valuable results by chance or miracle, or to deny, that their results have value.

But on the modern conception of art, this inability to 'render the reason'[1] of a work of art is a sign of its superiority. Dividing the arts into the fine and the useful, the creative and the mechanical, we recognize the conception of Techne as adequate to the latter only. To these it is genuinely adequate.[2] The craftsman can produce a useful

[1] λόγον δοῦναι.

[2] I think this assertion is true enough to serve as an illustration, but it is not entirely true. The conception of useful art has itself suffered a conversion no less than that of fine art, and the activity of the artisan is no more than that of the artist any longer exhausted in his being a Demiurge. As the technique of the latter is subordinated to an imaginative, so the technique of the former to an economic activity. This is that which was recognized by Plato himself as χρηματιστική but by him wrongly called a τέχνη, whereas it lacks both characters of a

object only on the strength of a previous understanding of the purpose which it is to serve, and the understanding of this purpose governs the whole of his activity. The purpose is the essence of the object when made, distinguishable by the understanding from its accidental qualities; and it is at the same time the ideal, the distinct conception of which alone qualifies the critic to judge this or that individual specimen to be good or bad. It remains to add that this intelligible form, which is purpose, essence, or ideal according to the point of view from which it is regarded, is specific and not individual.

Of the work of fine art none of these things is true. It is a commonplace that the artist does not execute according to a preconceived plan, and it is recognized as a vice of criticism when the critic judges by a standard conceived in distinction from the individual work. No distinction can be made between the idea, as essential, and the accidents of its embodiment.[1]

The significant thing is that these characteristics of the work of fine art are now recognized[2] as the signs of its

τέχνη, both that of being informative and that of being governed by a conceived idea. It is, on the contrary, both blind in its working, and creative in its result: the production of wealth. Plato's craftsman had his place assigned him in the Polis in virtue of his character as Demiurge. It was his function as a man to inform materials, and his function as a citizen to submit himself as matter to a similar information. All those modern theories, such as the Marxist, which have reversed the Platonic conclusion that the artisan is naturally subject, have been based upon the revised conception, according to which his essential activity is conceived to be not the technical, but the economic to which that is subordinate. Supremacy is claimed for the worker not because he is a skilled craftsman, but because he is a creator of wealth.

[1] That this distinction is possible in an allegory is the exception which proves the rule, since allegory is clearly a bastard form of art. It is recognized as a gross lapse of judgement to endeavour to interpret a genuine work of art as though it were an allegory.

[2] I suppose the opposition between these two conceptions of art was the main point at issue in the dispute between Classicists and Roman-

superiority, because they are the characteristics which belong necessarily to an activity of creation. The act of creation is governed by no preconceived end; therefore essence is not discernible from accident within the product of creation, and the created object, though it can be criticized, is not to be criticized by reference to a standard conceived apart from it.

It is not strictly accurate to say that information has been *displaced* by creation in the modern conception of art. It would be truer to say that it has been subordinated to it. No human activity is one of pure creation. Every artist requires some materials which he procures and does not make, and in reference to which his activity is one of information only. The information of his materials is his *technique*, but this, though an indispensable, is only a subordinate part of his activity. Technical skill does not make him a great artist, nor does technical perfection confer a genuinely aesthetic value upon his work. He is a great artist in virtue of the activity of imagination, of which the technical process is only the vehicle, and his work has value in virtue of what the imaginative activity creates.

It is significant that 'technique' is derived from the Greek word Techne. In this is preserved the conception of the activity which constituted in Greek theory the whole of

ticists. I may perhaps add that this change of idea has affected the practice and not only the theory of art. The elements of information and creation are mixed in different proportions in different arts. In such an art as sculpture the element of information is at its maximum, and at its minimum in such an art as music. It is hardly an accident that sculpture and music are peculiarly characteristic, the one of Greek and the other of modern artistic production. The remarks which I made on the relation of technique to imagination find their clearest example in the art of painting, which falls in this respect between the two extremes of sculpture and music, and to which indeed the term 'art' has been in large measure appropriated by linguistic usage. The art of literature raises some peculiar problems, because language, which is the author's material, is not a natural material.

art.[1] The essence of the modern conception of art is that in it the notion of information is (not effaced, but) subordinated to an activity which is not informative but creative.

A transformation has taken place in the conception of political in some respects analogous to that which we have sketched in the conception of artistic activity. As in the latter the idea of Techne, so in the former the idea of government has been preserved, but preserved as a subordinate part, not as the whole of political action. The concept of government includes almost all that was contained in the Platonic concept of ruling; it is an activity determined towards an end and directed by knowledge, it is informative and presupposes as its matter a body of those who are governed but do not govern. But here the resemblance ends. The government is not the supreme authority in the modern State as the ruler is in the Platonic Polis, but is subordinate to something of which Plato did not possess the conception: a sovereign *will*. The presence of sovereign will in a state makes only relative the subordination of subject to ruler, which all government entails, and which for Plato had been absolute. This is true though sovereignty be embodied, as Hobbes conceived it, in a monarch or an assembly, since it reduces governor and governed to an equality of subjection. The governor himself is only a minister or servant of the sovereign. And when sovereignty is held to reside in the people, then the subject of government is himself conceived as the source of that very authority to which he is submitted.

The organs of the sovereign will in a democratic State are those which we remarked in the previous chapter[2] to be typically English: Free Speech, Press, Party, Universal Suffrage, and Representation. The essence of these, in the

[1] Technique shares with τέχνη in particular the characteristic of being teachable. [2] Ch. V, pp. 168 ff. *sup.*

English conception of them, is not to be organs of government. They are not the means by which the ruler exercises power upon the subject, but the means by which the sovereign exercises power upon the ruler.

The sovereign will commands the law and constitutes the State. It displays the two characteristics of the creative will: that it is directed upon no end and hence not submitted to reason; that in constituting the State it creates, or brings into being something which had no natural existence.[1]

The State, which is the product of the sovereign will, possesses the characteristic of all created things, that its essence is not distinguishable. As no purpose determines the process of its making, the philosopher cannot understand it by discrimination of its essence nor the critic judge it by reference to its idea. It follows that there can be no metaphysical theory of the State, and no valid judgement of it by reference to a timeless standard. This does not of course mean that the State is above criticism and beyond understanding, any more than a poem is; it means that it is susceptible only of an historical understanding and liable only to an historical judgement.

Turning to consider the position of Hegel in regard to this development, we must observe, first, that he does not possess the fundamental notion that the State is the creation of a sovereign will. A State is not for him sovereign in virtue of the expression within it of a will which stands above its laws and creates its constitution, but in virtue of an organic unity.

Sovereignty is for Hegel that which makes the State in

[1] To have comprehended the nature of the sovereign will as creative is the especial merit of English Empiricism, and both of these characteristics are expressed by Hobbes, the former when he denies that the sovereign is subject to Laws of Nature, the latter when he asserts that the State is not natural but 'artificial'.

RULER AND SOVEREIGN

its external relation,[1] a unit, in its internal relation[2] a unity. In the former it entails the independence of the State of any power without it, in the latter the supremacy of the State over any power within it. In the latter relation, which we have principally to consider, Hegel's favourite expression is that the sovereignty of the State represents the 'ideality' of its constituent parts,[3] and it is necessary to explain as clearly as possible the meaning of this term.

The 'ideality' of its constituent parts is what differentiates an organism from an inorganic body, constituting them not parts, but members,[4] or organs. An organ is different from a part in that its essence is relative to the whole which includes it,[5] and that it can realize its own perfection only in performing its function in the whole. The domination of the whole over the action of its constituent members is the life of the organism; perfection of it is health and diminution of it is disease. Disease, according to Hegel[6] consists in the partial emancipation of one organ of the body from this control, so that it begins a life and development of its own. In doing this, the organ not only destroys the perfection of the whole, it loses its own perfection in precisely the same degree, failing to that extent to be what it is its essence to be. In an organism there can be no conflict between the interest of the part and that of the whole, because the proper being of the part is to be an organ of the whole and its proper activity to perform a function within it.

[1] 'Die Souveränetät gegen außen', §§ 321-3.
[2] 'Die Souveränetät nach innen', §§ 276-9.
[3] 'Die substantielle Einheit als Idealität seiner Momente.' § 276. 'Der Idealismus, der die Souveränetät ausmacht . . .' § 278 A. 'Das Moment der Idealität der besonderen Sphären und Geschäfte,' ibid. 'Die Idealität, nach welcher die inneren Staatsgewalten organische Momente des Ganzen sind.' § 324 A.   [4] § 278 A.
[5] As, in Aristotle's example, an arm ceases to be an arm when it is severed from the body.   [6] § 278 A.

According to Hegel sovereignty in the State is the same as life in an organism.[1] The organs of the State are the powers of government and the institutions of society, and there is no sovereignty (indeed there is no State) unless these are all subservient to the absolute authority of a single power. Hegel regards the Feudal Monarchy as the example of a society which has no sovereignty 'nach innen',[2] because there was no supreme authority within it, but each office and corporation in it had its own absolute rights and independent powers. It was thus precisely in the condition of the unhealthy organism whose members seek each its own development and are not limited to the performance of a function in the whole. Whereas the healthy State, like the healthy body, must be that in which there is no recalcitrance of any organ to the information by the life of the whole.

It is important not to misunderstand this doctrine. It does not mean that a State becomes sovereign by the elevation of a single power or element within it to an absolute domination over the rest. This is indeed the negation of sovereignty, as it is the negation of the idea of an organism that the activities of the organs should be subordinated to the interests of *another organ*. No single power in the State is the source of sovereignty, any more than the health of a body is the function of a single organ within it.

There is nevertheless one power in Hegel's State which is specially appropriated to be, not indeed the source, but the ultimate vehicle of the actualization of sovereignty; that of the constitutional monarchy.[3] The unity of the State is realized only in act, whether the waging of a war or such an

[1] § 278 A.   [2] Ibid.
[3] §§ 279-81, cf. '... der Subjektivität, ... welche den Begriff der fürstlichen Gewalt ausmacht, und welche *als Idealität des Ganzen* in dem Bisherigen noch nicht zu ihrem Rechte und Dasein gekommen ist' (§ 320. My italics.) 'Die Subjektivität des Monarchen ... soll ... die Idealität sein, die sich über das Ganze ausgießt' (ibid. z).

RULER AND SOVEREIGN

act as the abolition of slavery. The will to fight becomes an act through the *declaration* of war, the will to abolish slavery by the *proclamation* of its abolition. This final step in the passage from will to act can be taken only by an individual, and it is the function of the monarch to take it. He has to sink his individual personality, and to confine himself to giving final expression to a movement of will which he does nothing to initiate.[1]

Hegel differs from Hobbes in his conception of what sovereignty is, not simply in holding a different doctrine of the place where it resides. It must not be supposed that the contrast between the impotence of Hegel's monarch and the omnipotence of Hobbes' sovereign is due merely to the transference of sovereign power elsewhere within Hegel's State. Such a transference of sovereign power, say from king to people, would be easily compatible with Hobbes' conception of sovereignty, and would involve, of course, a similar reduction of the monarch to a status of comparative impotence. But the impotence of Hegel's monarch is not due to such a cause. That power to create law by willing it which Hobbes called sovereignty has not been transferred in Hegel's State to another holder than the monarch: it does not exist in Hegel's State at all.

We have remarked that the doctrine of Creation is the source from which the conception of sovereignty is derived. This doctrine is the fundamental doctrine of the Christian

[1] See the striking passage in § 280 z: 'Es ist bei einer vollendeten Organisation des Staats nur um die Spitze formellen Entscheidens zu tun und um eine natürliche Festigkeit gegen die Leidenschaft. Man fordert daher mit Unrecht objektive Eigenschaften an dem Monarchen; er hat nur Ja zu sagen, und den Punkt auf das I zu setzen. Denn die Spitze soll so sein, daß die Besonderheit des Charakters nicht das Bedeutende ist . . . In einer wohlgeordneten Monarchie kommt dem Gesetz allein die objektive Seite zu, welchem der Monarch nur das subjektive "Ich will" hinzuzusetzen hat.'

revelation, though of course the Christian revelation is by no means exhausted in it. That revelation as a whole is the source of almost all in modern philosophy that is distinctively modern; of almost all those characteristic features, for example, by which Hegel's own philosophy is differentiated from Plato's. But no modern philosophy[1] has absorbed the entirety of Christian doctrine. It has been the strength of modern Empiricism that it has founded itself firmly in all branches of speculation upon the truth of the doctrine of Creation, its weakness that it has failed to see that this fundamental truth is not therefore the whole truth. The Christian revelation itself begins, but does not close, with the Pentateuch. Of Hegel we may say on the contrary that he has assimilated the truth of many Christian doctrines, but not this fundamental one of Creation; so that he has grasped, as it were, consequential truths of Christianity, but not the premiss upon which they are based, and therefore not the consequences in their full significance.[2] This general judgement may be applied to his philosophy of the State.

Hobbes' thought is determined throughout by the presupposition that what is real is created, the natural by God's will, the artificial by man's. Both terms in the contrast of art with nature assume new meanings on this presupposition; nature now means created nature, and art creative art. So that when Hobbes asserts that the State is 'artificiall', he does not mean that it is the product of a Techne, but that it is a creation of human will. It was created by an act of will at the contract, and is sustained in being at each succeeding moment by exercise of a will itself similarly creative: the sovereign will.[3] Considered as product of the contract, the

---

[1] Still less any medieval one. [2] Cf. Ch. IV, p. 137 *sup*.
[3] As all created things require for their continued preservation the perpetual exercise of the same power by which they were initially

RULER AND SOVEREIGN

State is analogous to a product of creative art; considered as the product of the sovereign will, it is that and something more. The sovereign will is itself included in the State which it creates; the State is not merely created, but self-created by will, and thus, as *causa sui*, differentiated both from works of art and works of nature.

But the sovereignty of Hegel's State is not a product of will. Examination confirms what his terminology[1] betrays: that what he calls sovereignty is not anything essentially different from the natural unity which constitutes the life, and the strength of it the health, of an organism.

That is why the institutions of parliamentary democracy, of which it is the proper function to be organs (not of the enforcement, but) of the creation of the law, can find no place in Hegel's State; or rather can find a place in it only in so far as they are reduced from instruments of will to instruments of enlightenment. Since Hegel does not regard it as belonging to the nature of the State to contain within itself the power of creating itself, since indeed he lacks the conception of will as creative, he is bound, like Plato, to regard any exercise of will upon the law as perversive of its nature. Hence the solicitude with which he insists that these institutions must be denuded of effective power,[2] and that the act of legislation itself must not issue in the constitution of law, but only in the more detailed specification of a law in its general outlines preconstituted, and itself determining the legislative act.[3]

created. The sovereign will is related to the will of the contracting parties in regard to the State, as divine Providence to divine Creation in regard to nature.

[1] Constant use of the terms 'organism', 'organic' of the political constitution. Cf., e.g., §§ 256 A, 259, 267, 269, 271, 278 A, 286 A.

[2] Cf. Ch. V, pp. 178 ff. *sup*.

[3] 'Die gesetzgebende Gewalt betrifft die Gesetze als solche, *insofern sie weiterer Fortbestimmung bedürfen*, und die ihrem Inhalte nach ganz allgemeinen inneren Angelegenheiten. Diese Gewalt ist

But some implications of the premiss which he does not recognize are too strong for Hegel himself to resist them. He admits, in contradiction of his whole theory of 'Sittlichkeit', that it is a value in parliamentary institutions to subserve the expression of a will which is not conformed to reason;[1] that is, of a will which possesses all the characteristics of a creative will, except that it is carefully precluded from creating anything.

Nor is this all. In denying the right of the citizen to judge his State by reference to any standard conceived apart from it,[2] Hegel is attributing to the State the universal characteristic of *created* objects.[3] Thus one of the most famous of Hegel's own conclusions is the consequence of a premiss which he does not admit, and which, had he admitted it, would have entailed with equal necessity the further consequence that a philosophy of the State, which should rest upon the discrimination of essence from accident within it, was not possible.

In his doctrine of sovereignty, then, Hegel goes hardly any way, except in terminology, beyond Plato himself. Like Plato he sees the essence of the State in the unity of its members, and he does not do justice to the truth of the Hobbesian doctrine that a State must possess within itself the process of will of which its own unity is the product. Where Hegel most markedly differs from Plato is in his very insistence that the unity of the State is organic, that is to say, that it is a unity to be achieved in and through differentiation, and not by exclusion of difference. But in this he is differing from Plato not in conceiving the State as a more

selbst ein Teil der Verfassung, *welche ihr vorausgesetzt ist* und insofern an und für sich außer deren direkten Bestimmung liegt, aber in der Fortbildung der Gesetze und in dem fortschreitenden Charakter der allgemeinen Regierungsangelegenheiten ihre weitere Entwickelung erhält.' (§ 298. My italics.)

[1] Ch. V, p. 179 *sup.*
[2] Ch. V, pp. 172 ff. *sup.*
[3] pp. 185, 188 *sup.*

RULER AND SOVEREIGN

than natural unity, but in conceiving differently what is necessary to constitute a natural unity.

It may be said in general that Hegel reverts to the Greek doctrine that the State is 'natural' against the Hobbesian that it is 'artificial', but that his conception of the natural has been modified by the introduction into it of two important new elements: the first this of organism, the second that of evolution, which we have finally to consider.

When Hegel denies that the State 'is made', the contrary which he affirms is not that it 'is', but that it has 'come to be'.[1] It is 'natural', that is to say, not only in the sense in which the Platonic Polis is natural, that its idea has a timeless being in the nature of things, but in the further sense that it is the product of a natural development.

For a philosophy which does not possess the idea of creation, development is the temporal process of realization of an end, and is a process of art or of nature according as the end is or is not conceived as purpose by a human[2] mind, and as the means are or are not chosen by a human will as means to its achievement. The growth of a house from an architect's plan is an example of the former, the growth of a tree from a seed of the latter development. Plato had thought that his Polis could come to be only in the former manner, and he accepted the consequence that its realization must await a condition which might never be fulfilled: the birth of a statesman who should know the plan to be realized. Hegel was precluded from accepting this consequence by the most fundamental of his convictions, namely that the ideal State *is* realized. He was forced, therefore, to the adoption of the second alternative: that the State as it is in the present is the product of a

[1] Cf. § 298 z.
[2] The development remains natural if the end is conceived and the means are chosen by a *divine* Demiurge.

teleological process, of which the end was not conceived by any of the human agents whose acts were the means of its achievement.

This process is the process of World-history as it has unfolded itself up to the present time. It is a development, in that it is directed towards an end, and it is a natural development, in that the end is that of the 'Weltgeist' or World Spirit, which *uses* the human agents of history as unconscious tools to its achievement,[1] and which thus stands to them in somewhat the same relation as the divine Demiurge to processes of growth in nature. To be used thus by the World Spirit as a means to its end is what constitutes the historical importance of a people or of an event and the greatness of an individual.

These two conceptions of greatness and of historical importance were quite unknown to Greek philosophy, and Hegel's introduction of them marks an important step in the process of the assimilation by philosophy of other than Greek ideas. But it is significant that they are not introduced by Hegel into his philosophy of the State in the strictest sense, but only into the philosophy of history which the philosophy of the State presupposes.

Thus the will of the great man performs the essential function of the sovereign will: it brings into being the law which determines the activity of *every* power within the State, not only that of the government, but that of the legislature[2] and that of the monarch himself.[3] But it *is* not

[1] This is the famous doctrine of 'Die List der Vernunft'. See § 298 z for an illustration of how the selfish and ambitious acts of historical personages are turned to an end of which they had no conception. In § 344 the 'states, peoples, and individuals' who do the business of the World Spirit are called 'bewußtlose Werkzeuge', and in § 348 it is explicitly declared that the work which they do 'is concealed from them and is not their object or purpose'.

[2] § 298; quoted p. 193, n. 3, *sup*.

[3] § 280 z, quoted p. 191, n. 1, *sup*.

RULER AND SOVEREIGN

a sovereign will precisely because it lies outside the State which it constitutes. The task of the great men is ended when the State which they wrought unconsciously to achieve is completely realized. Hegel's State itself fails to be sovereign in the full and proper sense by lacking an organ to give expression to this will. It would acquire the character which Hobbes distinguished in his commonwealth by calling it 'artificial' only if the effective power of the great men of history were transferred to the 'political' will which Hegel condemns to futility, and expressed through the organs of parliamentary democracy which are atrophied in his State.

The will of the great man is different again in its nature from any of the five varieties of will which we have distinguished hitherto in Hegel's State.[1] It is like what we have called the 'political' will in that it can be subsumed under the concept of 'Sittlichkeit' by no possible accommodation in the definition of that term. The least which can be demanded of an act which is to be called 'sittlich' is that it shall be conformed to law, and the possibility of such an act presupposes upon Hegel's theory the previous embodiment in an historical State of the law to which it is to conform. But it is precisely this embodiment, the condition of future ethical acts, which the acts of great men result first in producing, and precisely its previous absence which dispenses them from the bonds of a rigid morality. But whereas the 'political' will is retained in the State at the price of being shorn of its practical efficacy, the will exercised by the great men retains its efficacy at the price of being excluded from the State.

Like the 'political' will, the will of the great man exhibits some of the characteristics proper to the creative will. The first of these is its independence of the guidance of

[1] Ch. V, p. 177 *sup.*

reason, emphasized by Hegel when he insists that the will of the great man is enlightened by no conception of the end which he is achieving. But perhaps more significant is the attribution to this will of the epithet 'great', since it seems true to say that greatness is to be attributed to a man, whether artist or statesman, in virtue of nothing else than his power of creation.[1]

It may indeed seem that the activity of the 'great men', as Hegel describes it, is one to which the epithet 'great' is not properly applied. Theirs is the passive role of an instrument, and they have no spontaneity in initiating the great works for which they are used. This is because Hegel, lacking the true notion of a creative will, has divided its characteristics between the will of the great men and the 'political' will, attributing to the former efficacy without spontaneity, and spontaneity but no efficacy to the latter. The creative will is realized only when both these characters are combined, as they are when sovereignty is attributed to the will expressed through parliamentary institutions, and it seems to have been the positive achievement of representative democracy to extend to all members of the

[1] It is consistent with this suggestion that the Greeks, lacking the idea of creation, lacked also the concept of greatness, and it is a sign of the extreme difficulty with which the notion of creation and its cognate conceptions have been assimilated into philosophical thought that even now there is hardly a philosopher, so far as I know, with the exception of Hegel himself, who has devoted serious consideration to the problem of greatness. Kant's theory of genius in the *Kritik der Urteilskraft* touches this problem so far as it concerns the creative artist. Among contemporary philosophers, Croce has mentioned the subject, but his assumption that greatness is the character of what he terms 'economic' activity seems clearly wrong. Quite recently the problems arising from the relation of greatness to goodness have been raised by Professor W. G. de Burgh ('On Historical Greatness', published in *Proceedings of the Aristotelian Society*, 1932, Supplementary Volume XI), with whose criticisms of Croce I agree, and with whom I have had the advantage of discussing the subject.

State some share, though slight and intermittent, in the same activity of creation in virtue of which a great man is called great.

William Cobbett expresses the principle at the root of parliamentary democracy when he says: 'Our rights in society are numerous, the right of enjoying life and property, the right of exerting our physical and mental powers in an innocent manner; but the great right of all, and without which there is in fact *no right*, is the right of *taking a part in the making of the laws by which we are governed*.'[1] The rights first mentioned are social rather than political. They require for their maintenance no more than the establishment of a just system of civil law. But the last one, the 'great right of all', is the right to a freedom[2] which can by its very nature be exercised only in so far as 'society' has become 'state'. Parliamentary institutions, including not merely Representation but all those other institutions which alone can make Representation effective, are in their essential nature means of realizing this participation of the subject in the making, that is to say, in the creation, of the laws by which he is governed; and those philosophers have understood but little of the nature of parliamentary democracy who have assumed that representation is no more than a device necessitated by the geographical extent of modern states, and thus only an inferior substitute for the primary assemblies of the Greek democratic cities.[3] The idea of a

[1] *Advice to Young Men*, vi, § 332.

[2] 'Disguise it how we may, *a slave*, a *real slave*, every man is who has no share in making the laws which he is compelled to obey.' Ibid. vi, § 332.

[3] 'Since all cannot, in a community exceeding a single small town, participate personally in any but some very minor portions of the public business, it follows that the ideal type of a perfect government must be representative.' J. S. Mill, *Representative Government*, ch. iii. (Mill's conclusion does not, in fact, follow from his premiss; the logical conclusion would be that the ideal type of a perfect government should be that of a single small town.)

representative system is not to perform ill what was performed perfectly in the city state, but to realize a freedom different in kind from any which it could enter the mind of a Greek to conceive. The freedom of the citizen of a Greek democracy consisted in his possession of an equal right with all his fellow citizens to rule, but not in the possession of a right to make the law which either he or another was bound as ruler to administer. On the Greek conception of ruling, the law could no more be made by the ruler than the science of medicine by the physician. But the franchise of the citizen of a parliamentary democracy does not confer a right either to rule or to participate in the activity of ruling; it confers the right to take part in the quite different activity, proper not to a ruler but to a sovereign, of commanding the laws which the ruler has to enforce.

This freedom is totally lacking to the citizen of Hegel's State.

The consequences in which Hegel is involved arise from his grasping the second horn of the dilemma,[1] that the State is the product either of an artificial or of a natural development, but the notion of creation, had he possessed it, might have enabled him to escape between the horns of it. If the only intelligible process is a teleological one, then the course of history, of which the State is the product, can be intelligible only if the human actions which compose it are directed to an end. Then there are only two alternatives: either the end is conceived as purpose by the individual human agents, or they are used as means to an end which they do not comprehend. They are either themselves the Demiurges of the State or instruments in the hands of a divine Demiurge, and there is no resource but to conceive them either as purposing what they do or as the unconscious tools of its achievement. To accept the former alternative

[1] Cf. p. 195 *sup*.

would be tantamount to maintaining that the course of past history has been, in fact, directed by the efforts of a series of philosopher-kings; and Hegel is driven to the second.

But once we break through the limitations of this whole Demiurge terminology, it appears that it is not necessary to regard the human agent either as an artificer or as a tool. To be unconscious beforehand of the end which he produces is the mark by which the creative artist is distinguished from the demiurge, and that the human agent in history is thus unconscious need not mark his degradation to the level of a tool so much as his elevation to that of a creator.

A work of creation is not intelligible in the same way in which a work of purposive information is, namely by distinct conception of its essence; but it is not therefore unintelligible. The difference in the two ways of understanding may be illustrated by comparing a product of informative with a product of creative art. A tool, say, or a machine becomes intelligible when the purpose which it serves is understood, and this purpose is object of a conception distinct from the sensuous experience of any particular example. A product of creative art may likewise be understood; the appreciation of a picture is something more than sensuous apprehension of the coloured surfaces of which it is composed. But it is not intelligible in the same way in which the tool is; that in it which makes it more than a conglomeration of coloured patches, its 'meaning' perhaps we may call it, cannot be made object of a conception distinct from the sensuous apprehension of these.

Somewhat similarly, a series of works of creation may be understood as a development, that is to say, as an intelligible series, without a distinct conception of an end to which they progress. In other words, there may be development in the created which is not teleological. This may be illustrated by the history of any creative art;[1] the painting, say, of one era may be understood to have developed out of that of the

It may be illustrated perhaps even better from the sphere of Biology. According to a pre-Darwinian theory, according to that of Malebranche e.g., the existing economy of living species in the world is to be understood as the end proposed to himself by God at the Creation, and the movements observed in organic nature as means to its achievement. Movement and change in the organic world was thus regarded as teleological, and as intelligible only to one who had comprehended the end. (The discovery of this end was the task set to themselves by pre-Darwinian naturalists in their search for the 'natural' classification of living species. Cf. *Encyclopaedia Britannica*, 11th ed., s.v. 'Zoology'.)

Malebranche himself combines this doctrine that process in nature is teleological with a belief in the fixity of species, but it is not essentially incompatible with a belief in the evolution of species. It might quite well be held that the divine plan for the distribution of species is *only now* or even *not yet* realized, and that the long process by which species have been or are still being modified and transmuted is itself a means to the ultimate achievement of an archetypal scheme which God purposed from the beginning. Such an evolution would be teleological, and would be like all teleological development intelligible only to one who understands the goal to which it moves, whether he holds that the goal is now achieved or that its achievement is reserved for the future.

Hegel regards the course of human history as such a teleological evolution. His 'Weltgeist' is related to human progress in the same way as divine Providence is related to animal development upon such a biological theory as we have sketched. (He holds the process to be now complete and the goal attained in the present.)

The revolutionary characteristic of modern biological theory (I shall continue to call it 'Darwinian', though without wishing to be committed to any estimate of Darwin's personal contribution to it) is not that it is based on the idea of an evolution of species, but that it is based on the idea of a non-teleological evolution of species. It assumes that the temporal succession of species is a development, but not in the sense that each succeeding one is the completer realization of an end which directs the development; it discriminates the higher from the lower, but not in the light of an ideal distinguishable from both.

This is only to say that the Darwinian biology attributes to natural species the kind of development which is proper to works of creation. Biology first under Darwin adopted from the Christian religion the truth that animals are creatures. His orthodox predecessors had believed this, but the belief had not penetrated their science. They had declared in their creeds that the kingdom of nature is the work of

RULER AND SOVEREIGN

era preceding it, without being understood as a nearer approximation to a perfection or end conceived in distinction from either. Political history similarly, so far as it is the product of a creative activity in man, may be understood as a development, without being interpreted as a teleological process.

But Hegel, here as elsewhere, lacks insight into the significance of creation. Just as he can conceive no virtue in practical activity except in so far as it is governed by a concept, so he can conceive no process to be intelligible which is not teleological. If human history is a teleological process, then it is to be rendered intelligible by a conception of its end distinct from the empirical description of the events which are means to its achievement. Thus Hegel is led inevitably to his vicious distinction of Philosophy of History from the empirical science of history, the former having as its object the end, the latter the means of the historical process.[1]

If Hegel fails to recognize creation as a human activity, he fails equally to recognize it as a divine one. His whole doctrine of history may be said indeed to depend upon two facts, that he has absorbed into his philosophy the truth of the Christian doctrine of a divine Providence governing human affairs, and that he has failed to absorb the truth of the Christian doctrine of divine Creation. It is due to the

a Creator, but had continued to treat it in their science as though it were the work of a Demiurge.

The Hegelian Philosophy of History suffers from a defect similar to that of a pre-Darwinian theory of biological evolution, and for the same reason: that it has failed to assimilate the truth of the Christian doctrine of Creation.

[1] The vice of this distinction is now so universally recognized that further exposure of it may be spared. I am indebted specially to Croce's forceful criticisms of the doctrine. I need hardly add that Hegel's own practice often enough belies his theory and that there is much great History in what he calls his Philosophy of History.

former that he is enabled to maintain that the ideal State is real, without being bound, as Plato was, to postulate the unfulfilled condition that its idea should have been conceived by the men who made it. It is the latter failure which is the root of the difficulties connected with the doctrine of the 'Weltgeist' and of the Philosophy of History. The 'Weltgeist', in a word, represents a Providence, but the Providence of a divine Demiurge, not of a divine Creator. Thus the human agent through which it works is related to it as tool to artificer; thus, above all, it works by purpose to an end, so that the process which it directs is a teleological one, and the end, as in every product of a demiurge, can be discriminated in thought from the means by which it is achieved or the matter in which it is realized.

Hegel himself claims that his doctrine of the 'Weltgeist' is the philosophical, and therefore adequate apprehension of the same truth which is represented imaginatively and therefore inadequately in the religious doctrine of Providence. He regards it as a sign of the inadequacy of the religious imagery that those who hold it, while they assert that there is a plan of Providence, deny that the plan is knowable,[1] and he claims it as the business of philosophy to penetrate the mysteries which religion thus maintains to be inscrutable. But in this instance Hegel perverts the truth which he purports to be 'translating into the concept'. To say that the plan of Providence is inscrutable is, no doubt, an inadequate expression, but the truth which it expresses inadequately is not that God's plan is knowable, but that, as Creator and not Demiurge, God does not act according to a *plan* at all. Hegel is not really replacing religious imagery by conceptual apprehension of the truth which it contains; he is replacing the Christian idea of Creation by the Greek one of Techne.

[1] Cf. § 343 A.

GLOSSARY

The following is a list of Greek words used in the text, with their nearest English equivalents.

Andreia, courage.
Arche, rule.
Arete, virtue.
Chrematistike, money-making.
Demiurge, craftsman.
Dikaiosune, justice.
Doulos, -eia, slave, slavery.
Eidos, form, species.
Eleutheros, -ia, free, freedom.
Episteme, scientific knowledge.
Epithumetikon, To, the appetitive element (of the soul).
Epithumia, desire.
Hexis, acquired disposition, character.
Logistikon, To, the faculty of reason.
Logos, reason.
Muthos, myth.
Nomos, law.
Nomothetes, lawgiver.
Orthe Doxa, right belief.
Paideia, education.
Polis, city.
Sophia, wisdom.
Sophrosune, temperance.
Stasis, faction.
Techne, art, craft.
Thumoeides, To, the spirited element (of the soul).
Thumos, anger, spirit.

INDEX

[c.w. = contrasted with]

Andreia, 11, 53 ff., 66 ff., 92 ff., 127, 134.
Arete, 39, 48 ff.
Aristotle, 45 n., 58 n., 96 n., 116 n., 125, 132 n., 143, 189 n.
Art, 183 ff.
— c.w. nature, 30 ff., 192.
— fine, c.w. useful, 174 n., 184 ff., 201.
— *see also* s.v. Techne.
Augustine, 130 n.
Auxiliaries, 10 ff., 44 ff.

Belief, right, *see* s.v. Orthe Doxa.
Biology, 174 n., 202 n.

Censorship, 43.
Chrematistike, 59 ff., 76 ff., 84, 86.
Christianity, 59, 135 ff., 166, 181, 191 ff., 202 n.
Class, 46, 60, 64, 67, 97–8, 160 ff., 164–5.
— c.w. trade, 24, 28 ff., 64.
Cobbett, 145 n., 199.
Common sense, 134 ff.
Corporations, 157–8, 160.
Creation, 136 n., 138, 181, 191 ff.
— artistic, 183 ff.
Criticism, 176 n., 185.
Croce, B., 198 n., 203 n.

Darwin, 202 n.
De Burgh, W. G., 198 n.
Descartes, 26 n., 59.
Development, 195 ff., 201 ff.
Dialectic, 117, 137 ff.
— Hegelian, c.w. Platonic, 121 ff., 166.
Dikaiosune, 29, 32, Ch. II *passim*.
Division of Labour, 3, 9, 15, 22.
— c.w. division of classes, 28 ff., 36–7, 39 ff., 60.

Economic order of society, 33 ff., 63, 67, 78 n., 86, 142 ff., 148.
Education, 11 ff., 24, 44 ff., 70–1, 94–6, 125.

Empiricism, 56, 61 n., 78 n., 113, 140, 147, 166, 188 n., 192.
Encyclopaedia Britannica, 202 n.
'Enlightenment', the, 82, 172.
Ergon, 48–9.
Estates, 67.
Evolution, 174 n., 195 ff., 201 ff.
Expediency, 171.

Feudal system, 98 n., 190.
'First city' of the *Republic*, Ch. I *passim*, 39 ff.
Form, c.w. matter, 13 ff.
Freedom, Ch. II, 82.
— moral c.w. freedom of desire, 86 ff.
— pagan, 92 ff.
— 'ethical', 124 ff.
— 'economic', 129 ff.
— 'ethical', c.w. 'economic', 110, 151 ff.
— 'patriotic', 169 ff.
— 'political', 169, 176 ff.
— of making laws, 199–200
— of speech and of the Press, 168, 176 ff., 187–8.

'Gemüt', 127.
'Gesetz', 113, 119; *see* s.v. Law.
Government, c.w. Monarchy and Parliament, 168.
— c.w. Sovereign, 187 ff
Greatness, 196 ff.

History, 118, 133, 174 n.
— philosophy of, 196, 203.
Hobbes, 26, 47, 61 n., 113 n., 114, 144, 147, 151, 165, 187, 188 n., 191.
Hypocrisy, 88, 166.

'Idealität', 189.
Individual, c.w. universal, 35, 171.

Justice, 34.
— in *Republic*, see s.v. Dikaiosune.

INDEX

Kant, 16 n., 34, 57, 61 n., 83–4, 86, 140, 156 n., 198 n.
Kroner, R., 138 n.

Law, Ch. IV.
— c.w. Nomos, 113 ff., 120, 130 n., 137 ff.
— c.w. Form, 111 ff.
— positive, 114, 117 ff., 134 ff.
— as command, 113 ff.
— as 'Gesetz', 119 ff.
— civil c.w. economic, 146 ff.
— natural, *see* s.v. nature.
Liberalism, 148.
Locke, 33, 34, 140, 143 n., 147, 148, 151.
Logos, c.w. To Logistikon, 58, 73.
— c.w. Muthos, 142.

Malebranche, 202 n.
Marxism, 184 n.
'Medicinal Lie', 43.
Mill, J. S., 199 n.
Monarchy, 168, 190 ff.
Moore, G. E., 135 n.
Morality (Kantian), 83, 86 ff., 108, 110 ff., 126.

Nature, 3 n.
— state of, 33, 143 ff.
— laws of, 33, 67, 145 ff.
Nomos, c.w. Law, 111 ff.

Ontological argument, 26.
Oracles, 97.
Organic unity, 2 ff.
— — of the Polis, 5 ff.; cf. 15.
— — of the State, 188 ff., 193 n.
Organism, 14–15, 189–90.
Orthe Doxa, 66, 94, 114 n., 123.

Paganism, 56, 96.
Parliament, 168.
Parliamentary democracy, 193, 198–9.
'Parts of the Soul', 51 ff., 74.
Party, 80 n., 168, 187–8.
Patriotism, 169 ff., 174 n.
Police, 157, 160.
Political association, nature of, 1–4, 13 ff., 30 ff., 40–1, 163 ff., 182.
Property, 84–5.

Providence, 192 n., 202 n., 203–4.
Public opinion, 168, 176 ff.
Punishment, 43–4.

Rationalism, 56, 61 n., 117, 147.
'Recht', 'das abstrakte', 146 n., 150.
Representation, 168, 187–8.
Roman Law, 33, 120.
Rousseau, 26 n., 57.
Rulers, in *Republic*, distinguished from Auxiliaries, 9 ff.
Ruling, a Techne, 18 ff., 28 ff., 41, 182–3, 200.

'Sittlichkeit', 89.
— of the Polis, contrasted with that of the State, 91 ff., 99–101.
Slavery, 45 n., 55, 56, 63 n., 97–8, 116.
Society, c.w. State, Ch. V.
Sophia, 12, 47, 56 ff., 74–5, 83, 123 ff.
Sophrosune, 99–101.
Sovereignty, 25, 187 ff.
Specialization, *see* s.v. Division of Labour.
Spinoza, 16 n., 143 n.
Spirit, 3 n., 26 ff., 40.
Stasis, 80 n.
State, c.w. Polis, Ch. I.
— c.w. Society, 33, Ch. V.
Stoicism, 56.
Subjectivity, Ch. III, App. E.

Techne, 8, 18 n., 180 ff., 183 ff.
— of ruling, *see* s.v. Ruling.
Teleology, 195 ff., 200 ff., 202 n.; *and see* s.v. Techne.
Trinity, doctrine of, 138 ff.

Universal, as Form c.w. Law, 111 ff.
— c.w. individual, 35, 171.

War, 8, 35 ff.
'Weltgeist', 196, 202 n.
Will, 131 ff., 177 ff.
— 'ethical', 124 ff.
— 'economic', 129 ff.
— 'ethical' c.w. 'economic', 110, 153, 161 n.
— *see also* s.v. Freedom.

PRINTED IN
GREAT BRITAIN
AT THE
UNIVERSITY PRESS
OXFORD
BY
JOHN JOHNSON
PRINTER
TO THE
UNIVERSITY

Titles in This Series

Adams, George Plimpton, see Gray, J. Glenn

1

Baillie, Sir James Black
The Origin and Significance of Hegel's Logic
(London, 1901)

2

Baillie, Sir James Black
An Outline of the Idealistic Construction of Experience
(London, 1906)

3

Croce, Benedetto
What Is Living and What Is Dead of the Philosophy of Hegel
(Translated by Douglas Ainslie, London, 1915)

4

Cunningham, Gustavus Watts
Thought and Reality in Hegel's System
(New York, 1910)

5

Foster, M. B.
The Political Philosophies of Plato and Hegel
(Oxford, 1935)

6

Gray, J. Glenn
Hegel's Hellenic Ideal
(New York, 1941)

bound with

Adams, George Plimpton
The Mystical Element in Hegel's Early Theological Writings
(Berkeley, California: University of California Publications
in Philosophy, vol. 2, no. 4, Sept. 24, 1910, pp. 67–102)

7

Haldar, Hiralal
Neo-Hegelianism
(London, 1927)

8

Harris, William T.
*Hegel's Logic. A Book on the Genesis of the Categories
of the Mind*
(Chicago, 1890)

9

Hegel, Georg Wilhelm Friedrich
Political Writings
(Oxford, 1964)

10

Hibben, John Grier
Hegel's Logic: An Essay in Interpretation
(New York, 1902)

11

Löwith, Karl
From Hegel to Nietzsche
(New York, 1964)

12

McTaggart, John McTaggart Ellis
Studies in Hegelian Cosmology
(Cambridge, 1901)

13

Niel, Henri
De la Médiation dans la philosophie de Hegel
(Paris, 1945)

14

Stirling, James Hutchison
What Is Thought?
(Edinburgh, 1900)

15

Wahl, Jean
Le Malheur de la conscience dans la philosophie de Hegel
(Paris, 1951)

16

Walsh, W. H.
Hegelian Ethics
(London, 1969)